INSTITUTE OF LEADERSHIP & MANAGEMENT

# SUPERSERIES

# Controlling Physical Resources

FOURTH EDITION

Published for the
Institute of Leadership & Management by **Pergamon** *Flexible* **Learning**

OXFORD   AMSTERDAM   BOSTON   LONDON   NEW YORK   PARIS
SAN DIEGO   SAN FRANCISCO   SINGAPORE   SYDNEY   TOKYO

Pergamon Flexible Learning
An imprint of Elsevier Science
Linacre House, Jordan Hill, Oxford OX2 8DP
200 Wheeler Road, Burlington, MA 01803

First published 1986
Second edition 1991
Third edition 1997
Fourth edition 2003

Copyright © 1986, 1991, 1997, 2003, ILM
All rights reserved.

No part of this publication may be reproduced in any material form (including
photocopying or storing in any medium by electronic means and whether
or not transiently or incidentally to some other use of this publication) without
the written permission of the copyright holder except in accordance with the
provisions of the Copyright, Designs and Patents Act 1988 or under the terms
of a licence issued by the Copyright Licensing Agency Ltd, 90 Tottenham Court Road, London,
England W1T 4LP. Applications for the copyright holder's written
permission to reproduce any part of this publication should be addressed
to the publisher

**British Library Cataloguing in Publication Data**
A catalogue record for this book is available from the British Library

ISBN 0 7506 5886 X

---

For information on Pergamon Flexible Learning
visit our website at www.bh.com/pergamonfl

---

Institute of Leadership & Management
registered office
1 Giltspur Street
London
EC1A 9DD
Telephone 020 7294 3053
www.i-l-m.com
ILM is a part of the City & Guilds Group

---

The views expressed in this work are those of the authors and do
not necessarily reflect those of the Institute of Leadership &
Management or of the publisher

Authors: Joe Johnson and Colin Everson
Editor: Heather Sergeant
Editorial management: Genesys, www.genesys-consultants.com
Composition by Genesis Typesetting Limited, Rochester, Kent
Printed and bound in Great Britain by MPG Books, Bodmin

# Contents

## Workbook introduction    v

1. ILM Super Series study links    v
2. Links to ILM qualifications    v
3. Links to S/NVQs in managemnent    vi
4. Workbook objectives    vi
5. Activity planner    vii

## Session A    Dealing with resources    1

1. Introduction    1
2. The organization's resources    1
3. Managing resources    5
4. People as a resource    8
5. Equipment as a resource    14
6. Land and buildings as a resource    16
7. Materials as a resource    17
8. Summary    21

## Session B    Storing and allocating materials    23

1. Introduction    23
2. The basic principles of stock control    24
3. Rotating stock    27
4. Managing stock    29
5. Receiving goods    37
6. Issuing goods    43
7. Stock levels    46
8. Computerized systems    48
9. Summary    55

## Session C    Purchasing, resource planning and security    57

1. Introduction    57
2. The purchasing function    58
3. Materials planning    65

## Contents

| | | |
|---|---|---|
| 4 | Resource planning and management | 70 |
| 5 | Security | 75 |
| 6 | Summary | 96 |

## Performance checks   97

| | | |
|---|---|---|
| 1 | Quick quiz | 97 |
| 2 | Workbook assessment | 100 |
| 3 | Work-based assignment | 101 |

## Reflect and review   103

| | | |
|---|---|---|
| 1 | Reflect and review | 103 |
| 2 | Action plan | 106 |
| 3 | Extensions | 108 |
| 4 | Answers to self-assessment questions | 113 |
| 5 | Answers to activities | 117 |
| 6 | Answers to the quick quiz | 119 |
| 7 | Certificate | 120 |

# Workbook introduction

## 1 ILM Super Series study links

This workbook addresses the issues of *Controlling Physical Resources*. Should you wish to extend your study to other Super Series workbooks covering related or different subject areas, you will find a comprehensive list at the back of this book.

## 2 Links to ILM Qualifications

This workbook relates to the following learning outcomes in segments from the ILM Level 3 Introductory Certificate in First Line Management and the Level 3 Certificate in First Line Management.

C6.4 Materials
1 Contribute to the timely supply of materials for operations.
2 Maintain a suitable system for storage of materials.
3 Apply an effective system for controlling the receipt and issue of materials.
4 Maintain records of material movements and stock.

C6.7 Security
1 Identify ways of ensuring security in the workplace.
2 Minimize risks to personnel, stock, equipment and data.
3 Make recommendations for reduction of risk to workplace security.

**Workbook introduction**

# 3 Links to S/NVQs in Management

This workbook relates to the following elements of the Management Standards, which are used in S/NVQs in Management, as well as a range of other S/NVQs.

B1.2   Contribute to the control of resources.

It will also help you to develop the following Personal Competences:

- communicating;
- focusing on results;
- thinking and taking decisions.

# 4 Workbook objectives

All managers have resources at their disposal. It is the way these resources are used and organized that shows up the differences between a good manager and an ordinary one.

Poor managers will continually bemoan their lack of resources. 'If only I had more people (or more time, or more information, or better materials and equipment),' they will say, 'I could do a decent job'. The response to such a complaint is invariably along the lines of:

**'The point is: what kind of job can you do with the resources you already have?'**

This workbook is all about the management and control of resources. To control a resource, you have to monitor how well its actual performance compares with the planned performance. Managing includes determining objectives and making plans.

### Workbook introduction

We will start by reviewing the types of resource and make a list of nine although, as we discuss, there are various ways of categorizing resources. We'll then consider four in more detail: people; land and buildings; equipment; and materials.

Sessions B and C focus mainly on materials, and especially the problems entailed in the acquisition and storage of these resources. Session B deals with the principles of stock control, rotating and managing stock, the receipt and issue of materials, and stock levels.
In Session C, we concentrate on the purchasing function, planning aspects of materials management, some examples of applied technology in this area, and the security of stock.

## 4.1 Objectives

When you have completed this workbook you will be better able to:

- contribute to the management and control of resources in your organization;
- explain the principles, and some ways of solving the problems, of stores and stock control;
- increase your skills in various aspects of materials management;
- identify risks to physical, human and information resources and have gained some practical ideas and experience with which to guard against them.

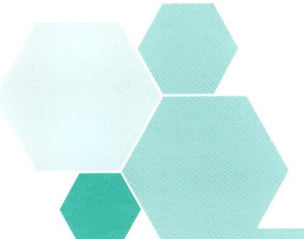

## 5 Activity planner

The following Activities require some planning, so you may want to look at these now.

- In Activity 2 you are asked to consider the way you monitor two specific resources and to suggest improvements in this area.
- Activity 5 asks you to explain how you might give individual team members more responsibility for the control of resources.
- For Activity 39, you will need to suggest a way of improving security in your area.

## Workbook introduction

Some or all of these Activities may provide the basis of evidence for your S/NVQ portfolio. All Portfolio Activities and the Work-based assignment are signposted with this icon.

The icon states the elements to which the Portfolio Activities and Work-based assignment relate.

The Work-based assignment involves putting forward a concrete proposal designed to reduce your organization's costs related to the management of materials.

# Session A
# Dealing with resources

## 1 Introduction

'Your role, as part of the management team – and never forget that that is what you are, and certainly in the eyes of your people – is to maximize the resources at your disposal to the full limits of your authority.'

John Adair, *The Effective Supervisor*[1]

Whether it's getting people to realize their full potential, making the most of limited time, getting work done in a restricted space, or avoiding the waste of energy, the organization of resources is largely what the job of management is all about.

In this session, we will discuss the background to our subject. We begin by classifying the resources used by all organizations.

Next, we consider the steps in the process of obtaining and managing resources, and then go on to review four specific kinds of resource: people; equipment; land and buildings; and materials.

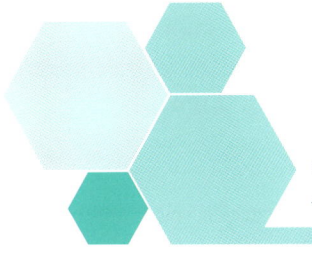

## 2 The organization's resources

A resource is a source of wealth. For organizations, resources are the means by which goods and services are produced.

[1] The Industrial Society, 1989.

**Session A**

## Activity 1

*3 mins*

Name **three** resources that you use in the course of your work.

_____

_____

_____


There are many kinds of resources, including:

- raw materials used in production processes – metals, plastics, fibres, and components of all kinds;
- machines used in making things;
- everyday materials for everyday activities, such as pens and pads;
- furniture;
- rooms, workshops and offices.

What about you – are you and your team a resource of the organization?

There are several ways to classify resources.

From the point of view of an economist, resources are classified into: land, capital, and labour.

- **Land** is the economic term used to describe all natural resources. Under this category would be included natural raw materials such as mined metals, and the ground on which work is done.
- **Capital** encompasses all non-natural resources, such as money, machinery, buildings and vehicles.
- **Labour** is a term for the human resources of an organization.

Another classification of organizational resources is: money, manpower, machines and materials – the four Ms.

However, it's useful to break down resources into rather more categories than either of these two groupings do. We will list nine different types of resource.

- Materials are components, raw materials (the inputs to a manufacturing process), consumables and other items upon which work may be done, or which aid people in doing work.

**Session A**

Every organization uses materials of some kind or other. Hospitals use syringes, bandages and blood. Caterers use foods and spices. Computer bureaux use disks, toner and paper. All materials cost money, and must usually be stored somewhere, ready for use.

- **Equipment is all the tools, machines, and other apparatus needed for making and measuring things, for protecting people, for handling information, for supplying power, and for many other applications.**

  Items of equipment range from safety helmets to desk-top computers to 600 megawatt generators. Two important points concerning equipment are that (a) it can be very expensive to buy and to run, and (b) it needs human expertise, if it is to be used well.

- **People are all the employees, including managers.**

  You may be surprised that we call people a resource. After all, people are the thinking, caring, decision-making, co-ordinating, hard-working animals known as human beings. Is it unfair to label them a resource? Certainly, like other resources, they cost money, and their services can be bought and sold. But we have to be careful not to treat people as if they were goods or simply a means of production; humans only respond well if you regard them as individuals and handle them with respect.

- **Buildings are, essentially, anything with a roof and walls.**

  Buildings – factories, offices, hospitals, barns, houses, schools, warehouses and so on – are usually the places where work is done and goods are stored. They are expensive, and take up a lot of space.

- **Land is where buildings are located, and where other work goes on.**

  Land is often in short supply, and can therefore be expensive to buy.

  (Note that to avoid confusion, we have separated land from buildings. However, in law, 'land' includes not only the surface, but the buildings on it, the ground below and the air above. And as already mentioned, the economist's definition of land is 'all natural resources'.)

- **Information is the knowledge or intelligence which tells us how to carry out work activities, whom to sell to, what to make, and so on.**

  The right information is often difficult to come by, especially at the time we need it. There is always plenty of useless information around, and a great deal of routine information that we need machines to help us process. It is often the best informed organizations that are the most successful.

## Session A

- Energy is the capacity to do work.

  We get energy from the sun, indirectly in the forms of oil, coal, other combustible matter, and nuclear materials, and directly as solar power. For most organizations, electricity (which is derived from one of the fuels just mentioned) is the main source of available energy. Of course, humans also need energy, which they get from food.

- Finance is the money and credit that are the funds of an organization.

  Without finance, few other resources could be obtained. An organization's funds may come from personal investments, bank loans, government loans or grants, and other sources. Limited companies issue shares to raise finance, and, in a public limited company (plc), these shares may be offered to the public.

- Time is the most elusive of resources.

  Time waits for nobody, is sometimes on our hands, and often flies. We may kill time, yet live to regret it, because we don't have enough of it. Not everyone would agree that time is a separate resource. 'If it is the time of humans we are concerned with,' they say, 'then it's part of the human resource.' But time, like other resources, can be managed, and used economically or wastefully.

So we have listed as resources:

- materials;
- equipment;
- people;
- buildings;
- land;
- information;
- energy;
- finance;
- time.

> We should distinguish between resources and **assets**. Not all assets are resources, and not all resources are assets. The word assets is an accounting term meaning: 'the property, together with claims against debtors, that an organization may apply to discharge its liabilities'.

In this workbook, we don't have room to cover all these resources in any depth, so we have some choices to make.

We will set aside the last four (information, energy, money, and time) and briefly review the others (people, equipment, land and buildings, and materials) in this session.

Then, in the next two sessions, we will focus mainly on the acquisition, storage, and allocation of materials and other physical resources.

But first, a word about the management of resources generally.

# 3 Managing resources

The management of resources involves the following:

1. deciding what you want to achieve

2. making plans to achieve it

3. specifying the necessary resources

4. locating and acquiring those resources

5. preparing the resources

6. controlling and organizing the resources to best effect.

The organization first needs to decide what it wants to achieve: what are its aims and objectives? There may be long-term and short-term objectives. A supermarket chain may have an overall objective to become bigger and more successful than all its rivals. Meanwhile, in the shorter term, it may decide to open three new branches, and so must then plan to acquire the land, buildings, equipment and people necessary for this aim.

The detail of these plans will include precise specifications of all these resources. The organization must answer questions such as the following.

'What resources will exactly suit our needs?'

'To what extent can we afford to compromise, and make do with less than the ideal?'

'Where can these resources be obtained?'

'How much money are we able and willing to spend on each resource?'

Once the resources are acquired, they must be prepared for use. The preparation will obviously vary according to the type and condition of the resource. Land may have to be cleared, buildings renovated, people trained and equipment set up.

Then, once ready, the resources will have to be organized and controlled, in order to get the best from them.

**Session A**

## 3.1 Monitoring resources

You may be involved in all the steps listed above, but much of your job may consist of controlling resources – the last step. A key part of controlling is in **monitoring** their use.

You have to know, to a more or less detailed level, about the **quantity**, **quality** and **cost** of the resources under your control.

Doing this job well necessitates:

- keeping in close touch with what your team members are doing: how well they are coping, what problems they are encountering, and so on;
- knowing whether the equipment your team needs is available, and in good working order;
- being informed about the materials being used: whether they are in good supply, of the right quality, and are being used efficiently;
- ensuring that the available workspace is used effectively.

## Activity 2

15 mins

S/NVQ B1.2

This Activity may provide the basis of appropriate evidence for your S/NVQ portfolio. If you are intending to take this course of action, it might be better to write your answers on separate sheets of paper.

Following on from Activity 1, be more specific about the resources you have responsibility for. Summarize them under the following headings.

People (e.g. how many, and in what capacities?).

**Session A**

Equipment (e.g. what types, and what level of value?).

_____
_____
_____
_____
_____

Materials (e.g. what kind, and what level of value?).

_____
_____
_____
_____
_____

Land and buildings, if any (e.g. what size areas?).

_____
_____
_____
_____
_____

Now think about the steps you take to monitor **two** specific resources under your control.

Specific resource 1: _____

How do you monitor the use of this resource, and at what intervals?

_____
_____
_____

If you identify a problem, what do you do about it, and whom do you notify?

_____
_____
_____

**Session A**

Specific resource 2: _____

How do you monitor the use of this resource, and at what intervals?

_____
_____
_____

If you identify a problem, what do you do about it, and whom do you notify?

Now suggest at least **one** way in which the monitoring of one of these resources could be improved. Be as detailed as you can in your answer.

_____
_____
_____
_____
_____
_____
_____
_____
_____
_____
_____

Now we will look at each of four resources in turn: people; equipment; land and buildings; materials.

## 4 People as a resource

There is sometimes some reluctance to see people as a resource. Hard-nosed senior managers may see them principally as a cost. Others may think that to regard people as a resource is to see them in the same way as materials or machines. But they **are** a resource and one that is critical to success.

**Session A**

## Activity 3

*3 mins*

How can an organization approach the problem of 'specifying' the people it needs?

_____
_____
_____
_____
_____

Most organizations will first decide on the jobs they want done, and the abilities they think are likely to be needed to do them. Generally, organizations are less likely to define personal attributes such as 'Must have brown hair, blue eyes, and good table manners', which could be discriminatory, in any case.

To that end, a job description or specification is normally drawn up. The organization then tries to attract candidates who are likely to be capable of doing that job competently. In many ways, the process isn't far different from buying a piece of equipment. You don't usually start by naming a particular supplier; instead, you decide what you want the equipment to do, and then see which equipment on offer would provide the best value.

But, even before any thought is given to acquiring new people, the organization must analyse objectives, and break the overall task into 'person-sized' pieces. For example, before a school can work out how many teachers it should employ, and with which skills, it will need to know:

- the number of pupils it is expecting to house;
- which subjects must be taught, and at what level;
- how many periods one teacher can cover in a week;

and so on.

With people, as with any other resource, it's a question of the following.

- What do we want to achieve?
- Which activities will help us get there?
- What resources are needed in order to carry out those activities?
- How can we get hold of those resources?
- How can we get the most from the resources once we have them?

9

**Session A**

In this brief discussion of people as a resource, we won't go into the subjects of interviewing, recruitment, training, motivation and other aspects of personnel management, which are covered in othe Super Series titles.

Instead, let's focus on some of the differences between people and other resources.

## 4.1 The under-used resource

People are probably the least well-developed resource. As John Harvey-Jones said in *All Together Now*[2]:

> 'I invariably challenge every company I visit by asking them what proportion of the capability of their people they think they are using. I have yet to meet a single one claiming that they are using as much as a half of their people's capabilities if they were released. We talk continuously about the need to improve our productivity and, God knows, it is a dire need; yet we appear to accept with equanimity that in the world of work we are achieving less than half of our capacity.'

### Activity 4 · 3 mins

If this observation is true, what explanation can you give for it? Why do you think organizations find it so hard to release the capabilities of people?

_____
_____
_____
_____
_____

Perhaps you referred back to the comments after the last Activity.

[2] Mandarin Paperbacks, 1995.

**Session A**

Organizations usually get people to fit the jobs, rather than making the jobs fit the people. That being so, employees can only use certain specific skills, and may have little opportunity to shine in other areas. For example, a child care worker may be a brilliant organizer, but may get paid mainly for his or her social skills, rather than administrative ones. Or a secretary with a flair for tactful negotiation may spend most of his or her time typing letters, because that's the job that needs to be done.

If the team leader or manager is perceptive enough to recognize under-developed or unused abilities in individual team members, the next problem is to find ways of using them. That's not often easy. There have been instances of organizations branching off in a new direction, when its management realized it had a pool of hidden talent in its midst, but these occasions are rare. You may have sometimes found yourself in the position of having to realize certain aims, and making the best use of available resources in doing so. The only options are in matching a given set of people to a given list of jobs; nothing else is on the agenda.

There are also other difficulties associated with developing people, including:

- the cost of arranging sufficient training, of the right quality;
- motivating individuals, so that they want to work hard and get better at what they do;
- ensuring that jobs are more challenging than boring, but without being too difficult or stressful;
- getting people at all levels involved with decision-making, and especially with making decisions about their own jobs.

This last point has been the subject of a great deal of discussion in recent years. You may have come across the word 'empowerment'. Broadly speaking, this means allowing teams and team members to decide the best way of getting their work done, rather than working under close management. The advantages, when empowerment has been carefully implemented and is properly supported, are increased motivation and efficiency.

**Session A**

## Activity 5

*15 mins*

**S/NVQ B1.2**

This Activity may provide the basis of appropriate evidence for your S/NVQ portfolio. If you are intending to take this course of action, it might be better to write your answers on separate sheets of paper.

Describe the ways in which you give your team members opportunities to take individual responsibility for the efficient use of resources.

Now explain how you might increase these opportunities.

If you were to give team members more individual responsibility, what effects do you expect it would have on efficiency and morale?

Session A

## 4.2 Treating people as individuals

Another major difference between people and other resources is that employees should never be regarded as simply a means to an end. Organizations that treat their people as if they were items of equipment, to be used and set aside at management's whim, will never get the best from this precious resource.

As Peter Drucker wrote:

> '... we habitually define the rank-and-file worker – as distinguished from the manager – as a man [sic] who does as he is directed, without responsibility or share in the decisions concerning his work or that of others. This indicates that we consider the rank-and-file worker in the same light as other material resources, and as far as his contribution to the enterprise is concerned as standing under the laws of mechanics. This is a serious misunderstanding.'[3]

These remarks are also relevant to Activity 4.

To avoid the mistake of regarding employees as objects, we have to realize that people don't come in bulk packages. Every person is unique, and has an individual contribution to make. Perhaps you think this is so obvious as not to be worth saying. If so, give truthful answers to the questions in the next Activity.

## Activity 6 · 2 mins

How does your organization treat temporary employees? If, say, you hire a clerk, a labourer, or a technician for a few days or weeks, is there any attempt to: (circle your response)

- get to know that person as an individual?  YES/NO
- treat the temporary employee with the same respect as permanent staff?  YES/NO
- give him or her as much support as other staff?  YES/NO
- regard the person as someone who needs motivation and job satisfaction?  YES/NO

[3] *The Practice of Management* (1999), Butterworth-Heinemann.

13

**Session A**

Perhaps you were able to answer 'yes' to all these questions. It is not unknown, however, for temporary employees (and permanent ones) to be regarded by management and other staff as if they were subhuman – things rather than people.

It would be easy to fill this workbook with discussions on the subject of people resource management, but that is not our main aim. We must move on to other topics.

# 5 Equipment as a resource

Equipment is a term encompassing various kinds of clothing, tools and machinery. It is by its nature technical, being based on one or more kinds of technology. The word 'technology' has itself been defined as:

**'the practical application of methods for using physical resources'.**

## Technology and competition

Now, even people with little technical knowledge recognize that technology is liable to become outdated very quickly. This fact poses many problems for work organizations. Because of competition, few organizations can afford to become complacent about their methods of producing goods or services, or the systems used in their internal processes. Every organization has to continually find new answers to the following questions.

- How can we raise our quality?
- How can we lower our costs?
- How can we improve our methods?
- How can we do things better than we are doing now?

The drive for increased efficiency and effectiveness often leads down the path of either new technology, or improved methods for utilizing existing technology.

Of course, highly technical and up-to-date equipment (such as automated assembly lines; supercomputers; body scanners and other sophisticated medical machinery) is invariably extremely expensive to purchase and to run. This may place organizations in the dilemma of not being able to afford the investment until income increases, and not being able to increase income until the new machinery is installed. The pooling of resources is often one solution, and this is sometimes part of the rationale behind company mergers.

*We'll look at some examples of the way in which technology is used in materials management, later in the workbook.*

**Session A**

## Equipment as a daily resource

Deciding what equipment to obtain, and when and how to obtain it, is one problem for managers. What about the day-to-day difficulties?

### Activity 7 — 4 mins

What problems do you encounter regarding the use and control of equipment in your area? EITHER list **three** or **four** different problems, OR describe **one** particular problem in detail.

As we have discussed, equipment is often both expensive and complex. As such, it needs a special kind of management. If you use the wrong equipment, or use it incorrectly, the result can be a disaster; at best it will make you and your team inefficient. Typical problems include:

- people not being trained to make the best use of equipment;
- machines and other equipment breaking down or becoming worn;
- having insufficient equipment;
- using inappropriate equipment;
- abusing equipment, deliberately or otherwise;
- using equipment incorrectly.

To get the optimum value from equipment, it is important for the people using it to have:

- a good understanding of what it is designed to do;
- training in how to use it;
- a proper system of maintenance;
- an appropriate system of security.

**Session A**

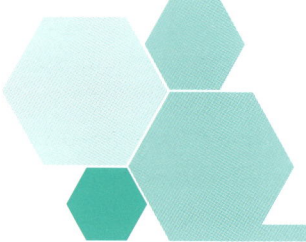

# 6 Land and buildings as a resource

Under English law, land and premises are held either as freehold or as leasehold estate.

When an organization purchases the **freehold** of a piece of land, it becomes the outright owner. With certain exceptions, it then owns everything beneath the surface and all the airspace above. If the value of the property rises, the freeholder benefits; if it falls, the freeholder may have to sell at a loss. Because they cost such a lot, and because owners are vulnerable to fluctuations in the property market, land and buildings require very careful management.

**Leasehold** property is held under the terms of a lease. This grants the leaseholder a right to occupy the land for a fixed period of time, typically for 99, 200 or 999 years.

Usually, the lease will impose restrictions on the use to which the land can be put. The landlord may also specify that repairs be carried out by the occupier, and that rates and taxes be paid.

Apart from the use of land to build upon, either to use or to sell, it may be a more direct source of wealth, for a mining or agricultural company, for example.

Although you may not be responsible for your organization's land and buildings, it is quite possible that you are in control of a work area that is part of a building or land resource.

## Activity 8 · 5 mins

Try to **list** three aspects you need to consider when managing a work area. To give you a start, equipment access is one consideration.

_____

_____

_____

16

You may have mentioned the following.

### Access to equipment

Where equipment is needed to carry out a task, it should be in a position where team members can get to it without hindrance. The workspace layout should be designed so that the most frequently used equipment is in the foreground, while rarely used items are further from the work area. Again, safety needs to be borne in mind: it can sometimes be unsafe to make equipment too accessible.

### Movement of people

For safety reasons, people need to be able to move about freely in their workplace. But they shouldn't find it necessary to make excessive or unnecessary movements, perhaps because materials and equipment are not close to hand. In addition, if individual paths cross too frequently, work processes may become slow and inefficient.

### Orderliness and appearance

A well-managed workspace will be free of clutter and dirt, in order (a) to make the work atmosphere more agreeable, and more productive; and (b) to reduce hazards from fire and accidents.

The overall appearance of the workplace will almost certainly have an effect on morale, and on the response of visitors. Polish and paint can work wonders in this regard.

### Siting of materials

As with equipment, thought needs to be given to the placing of work materials, with the efficiency of the workteam in mind.

### Grouping of staff

Should team members with similar types of expertise be situated together, or would 'skills mix' be more efficient? Different teams work in different ways, and each team leader has to consider which would be most effective.

## 7 Materials as a resource

In the remainder of this workbook, we will be discussing the storage, allocation, and acquisition of materials. Materials are sometimes subdivided into raw materials, components and consumables.

**Session A**

## Activity 9

*3 mins*

Of the materials you use in your workplace (some of which you may have listed in Activity 2), jot down the name of **one** type of consumable, **one** type of component and **one** type of raw material.

_____
_____
_____
_____
_____
_____
_____

**Consumables** are items that are used up in a work process, and do not necessarily form part of the final product. Examples are cleaning materials, glue, paper documents, masking tape, pens and pencils.

**Components** are parts, often having themselves been manufactured from raw materials, which go to make a larger assembly. One component of a door is its handle; some of the components of an electric lawn-mower are the rotating blades, the motor, the cable and the on-off switch; engines, wings and fuselage are all aircraft components.

**Raw materials** are basic substances that are processed in order to manufacture products. Paper is used to make books; silicon is a raw material in the manufacture of transistors; leather is a necessary material for many kinds of shoes; sheet metal is pressed and formed to make car bodies.

Of course, materials are needed in all organizations, not only manufacturing ones. Market gardeners use fertilizer and seeds; transport companies need vehicle spare parts, fuel and log books; financial advisers are likely to use lots of paper and printer toner; locksmiths have key blanks, oil and metal parts; county councils use large quantities of all kinds of materials.

The main problem usually associated with the management of materials is in getting them into the right place at the right time, while keeping costs to a minimum. This problem is the focus of our attention in the next two sessions.

**Session A**

# Self-assessment 1

*15 mins*

1 One classification of resources we discussed was their division into:

- land: the economic term used to describe all natural resources;
- capital: all non-natural resources;
- labour: a term for the human resources of an organization.

How would you match our later list of nine resources against these three? Answer by ticking the appropriate boxes in the table.

|         | Materials | Equipment | People | Buildings | Land | Information | Energy | Finance | Time |
|---------|-----------|-----------|--------|-----------|------|-------------|--------|---------|------|
| Land    |           |           |        |           |      |             |        |         |      |
| Capital |           |           |        |           |      |             |        |         |      |
| Labour  |           |           |        |           |      |             |        |         |      |

2 Fill in the blanks in the following list with suitable words.

The management of resources involves:

1 _____ what you want to achieve;

2 making _____ to achieve it;

3 _____ the necessary resources;

4 locating and _____ those resources;

5 _____ the resources;

6 _____ and organizing the resources to best effect.

**Session A**

3   Complete the following crossword by solving the clues. All the words in the answer were mentioned in the session.

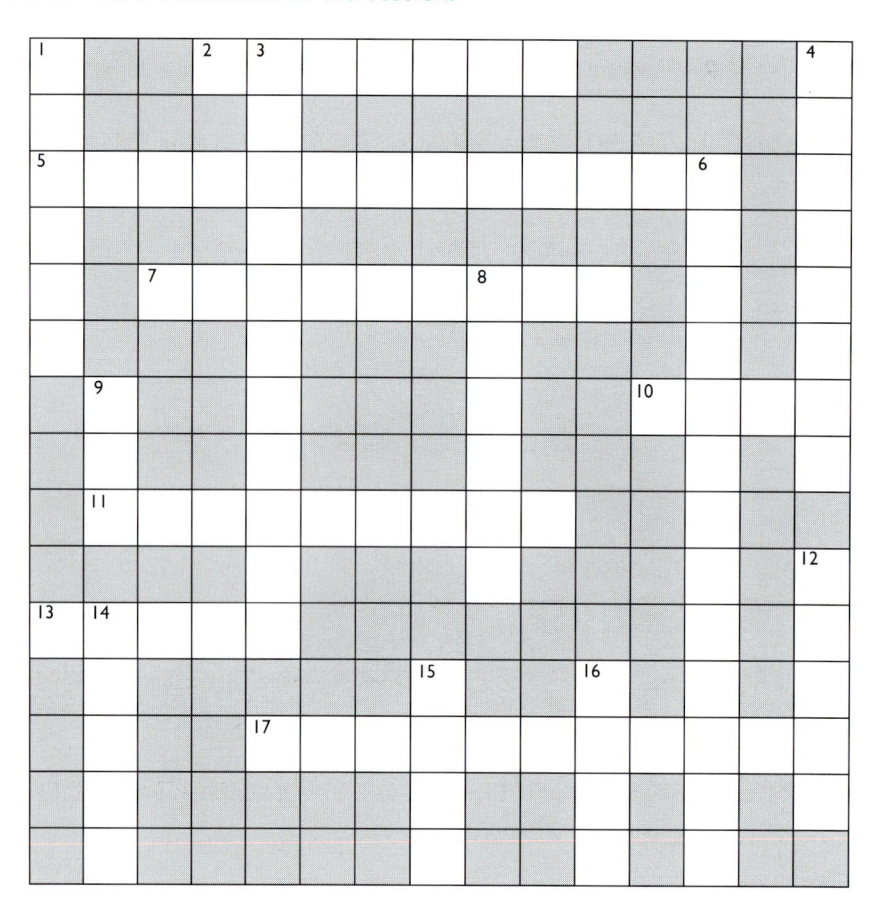

ACROSS
   2. Obtain (7 letters).
   5. Employment bodies (13 letters).
   7. Implements, machines, etc. (9 letters).
   10. We don't have enough of it, but we sometimes kill it (4 letters).
   11. Where organizations are housed (9 letters).
   13. These are useful for making things with (5 letters).
   17. There's plenty of this around, but often it's not of the right sort (11 letters).

DOWN
   1. A most precious resource (6 letters).
   3. Materials that can be used or eaten (11 letters).
   4. Resources are the means by which goods and _____ are produced (8 letters).
   6. Detailed description of what has to be done (13 letters).
   8. The capacity for activity or work (6 letters).
   9. Anything one has to do (3 letters).
   12. We sometimes make these things before we start work (5 letters).
   14. Land and other resources are _____ in short supply (5 letters).
   15. Labour, toil, effort or drudgery (4 letters).
   16. On which buildings are constructed (4 letters).

Answers to these questions can be found on pages 113–14.

# 8 Summary

- From the point of view of an economist, resources are classified into: land, capital and labour.

- We listed nine types of resource: materials; equipment; people; buildings; land; information; energy; finance; time.

- The management of resources involves:
  - deciding what we want to achieve;
  - making plans to achieve it;
  - specifying the necessary resources;
  - locating and acquiring those resources;
  - preparing the resources;
  - controlling and organizing the resources to best effect.

- Organizations usually acquire employees after first writing out a job description, defining the skills and other qualities that match the jobs to be done.

- People are frequently an under-developed resource. They are certainly special, and must be treated as individuals.

- To get the optimum value from equipment, it is important for the people using it to have:
  - a good understanding of what it is designed to do;
  - training in how to use it;
  - a proper system of maintenance;
  - an appropriate system of security.

- Although first line managers don't often have to take responsibility for land and buildings, they are often in control of a work area.

- Materials can be divided into raw materials, components and consumables. The main problem usually associated with the management of materials is in getting them into the right place at the right time, while keeping costs to a minimum.

# Session B
# Storing and allocating materials

## 1 Introduction

EXTENSION 1
See page 108 for details of Jessop and Morrison's useful book.

'The stores should be considered as a temporary location for materials needed for operational purposes, and should be planned, organized and operated in such a way that the period of residence of each item is as short as possible consistent with economic operation. The only reasons for carrying operating stocks is that the material is needed, and that supply cannot be exactly matched with demand.'

David Jessop and Alex Morrison, *Storage and Supply of Materials*

The storing of materials is not a subject that most people give a moment's thought to. A store does not seem to be an interesting place – it's just a location for holding things we want to use later. But for many, perhaps most, organizations, a store is a critical function: badly run, it can bring a company to its knees. The equation is simple: if you try to store too much, you will tie up money in materials unnecessarily, and clog up the stores area; if you try to store too little, the organization's work will be held up waiting for supplies.

We'll start this session with a discussion of the basic principles of stock control. Then we'll go on to the rotation and management of stock, the receipt and issuing of goods, and stock levels.

**Session B**

# 2 The basic principles of stock control

As we have discussed, all organizations need resources.

So far as materials are concerned, the problem is to get the correct goods, of the required quality, in the right place at the right time.

Obviously, planning is needed in order to achieve this. As these plans proceed, there will come a point when the following can be said.

**'We know exactly what we want, and when and where we want it. Now how can we get each specific item in the required place at the specified time?'**

Usually, it is the timing that is the most difficult part, and there are typically two ways of answering this question. A very large organization may be able to pass on the problem to its suppliers by using **just-in-time** methods. As we will discuss in Session C, the concept of just-in-time means that the organization is very specific in what it demands of its supplier.

**'We want you to supply these goods to a guaranteed level of quality, and to deliver them at precisely the time we can use them – not before or after.'**

However, most organizations do not use components and materials at a rate that can justify such a system. Instead they must buy, and take delivery of, materials in advance of when they are needed. They have to check them to see that the goods are of acceptable quality, and then keep them in **stock** by placing them in a storage area, where they can be held in good condition until they are wanted.

It follows that:

**stock is a buffer between supply and demand, or between the suppliers and the users.**

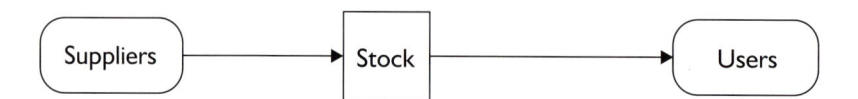

Suppliers → Stock → Users

**Session B**

## 2.1 The problems of holding stock

The first problem with holding stock is that it is an expense, not a source of profit. A retailer, for example, may have a large warehouse full of first-class merchandise; but it is of absolutely no use until it 'passes the till' and produces some income. Until then, it is a cost: the longer it stays in store, the bigger the cost.

### Activity 10

*4 mins*

What kinds of costs are incurred by keeping goods and materials in store? Try to think of **two** kinds of cost, and say when and how they are incurred.

_____
_____
_____
_____
_____

You may have noted the following points:

- The stock itself is not free: it has to be paid for. The money to pay for it comes from the firm's working capital, and as long as the goods are in store without being sold or used, that capital cannot be used for anything else. This is a nuisance, because that money could be doing something more useful, such as improving handling facilities or training the workforce. If the organization has had to borrow the capital that is tied up in stocks, the interest will have to be paid. If it is the firm's own money, it could have been earning interest.
- Stock needs space, and space costs money. Warehouses and stockrooms have to be designed and built; rent and rates may have to be paid. Racking, handling equipment and control systems have to be bought, installed and maintained. The more space used, the bigger the cost.
- There is also the work involved: the more stock, and the bigger the storage area, the more staff are needed to run and maintain it.
- You may also have thought of another reason why stocks are a cost and an expense: losses and deterioration. Even with the best-organized and best-designed storage facilities, there is a risk of them losing their value – usually

**Session B**

called **shrinkage**. The longer the stock remains in store, the greater the risk of losses from these causes. The main causes of shrinkage are:

- deterioration of quality;
- date-codes being passed;
- damage;
- pilferage;
- obsolescence.

## Activity 11

*3 mins*

How might a part be made useless through becoming obsolete (that is, going out of date)?

_____
_____
_____
_____

Some, for example the spare parts for old machines, may become useless when the machines are replaced. Others may become obsolete because there has been a change in the law, in industry standards, in a customer's specifications, or in market demands.

To sum up: for all the reasons we have discussed, organizations:

**aim to keep the minimum stocks in the minimum space for the minimum time.**

What can go wrong when this principle is applied? It is expensive to hold too much stock, but what is potentially even more damaging to an organization is that insufficient goods are available when they are needed. If this happens:

- work may come to a stop;
- people may be laid off;
- sales and customers may be lost.

**Having stocks too high is bad news; having stocks too low may be worse news.**

**Session B**

Clearly, stock control can be a very important activity for an organization.

Now let's look at stock control with these two main constraints in mind. First, we'll think about ways of reducing the costs of holding stock. One way to do this is to make sure that the oldest stock is used first.

# 3 Rotating stock

It is very important to make sure that all the goods kept in the stores are in good condition, and that they don't deteriorate or become damaged in any way. It obviously helps to use the oldest stock before the newest. By the 'oldest' we mean the goods that have been in stock the longest.

The technique that demonstrates this principle is referred to as:

**first in, first out (FIFO) or stock rotation.**

The idea is that the first consignment of a particular item to be received in the stores should also be the first to be issued. The benefits of this approach are that:

- space is made available for newer consignments being delivered;
- the average quality of the items in the store is as high as possible;
- older items do not get lost or hidden by newer items.

There will, of course, be times when it is necessary to use newer stock before old, perhaps because there might be small differences in the newer stocks that affect how they can be used. Nevertheless, FIFO rotation is an important principle for stores management.

A more important reason for rotating stock, however, is to help reduce costs. The oldest goods carry the oldest costs (and prices), and if these are issued before newer goods with higher prices, this will:

- help control the general level of costs
- keep the value of the stocks in line with their 'book' values.

**Session B**

## 3.1 The two-bin system

The simplest method of stock rotation is the 'two-bin system'. The term 'bin' is used in stores to refer to a particular part of a shelf or a container and, in many cases, a 'bin' may actually **be** a bin. The basis of the system is described in the figure below, and there are many variations to be found.

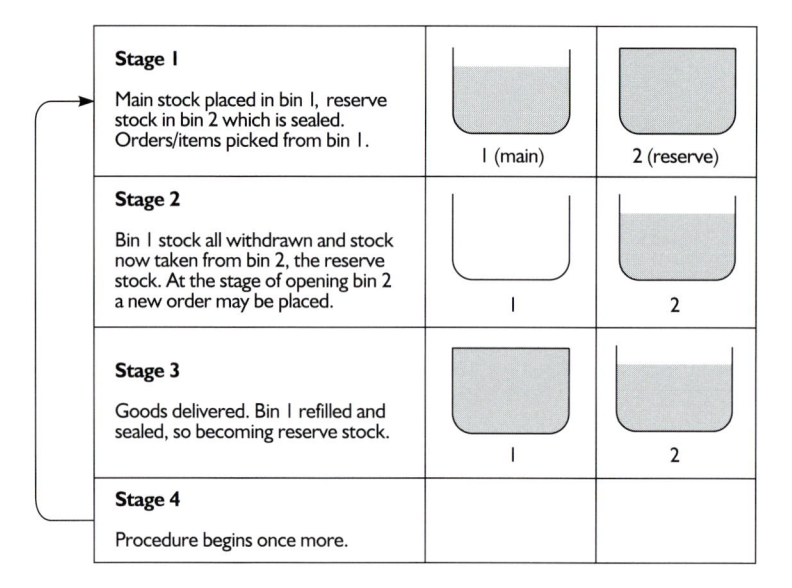

| Stage | Description | Bin 1 | Bin 2 |
|---|---|---|---|
| Stage 1 | Main stock placed in bin 1, reserve stock in bin 2 which is sealed. Orders/items picked from bin 1. | 1 (main) | 2 (reserve) |
| Stage 2 | Bin 1 stock all withdrawn and stock now taken from bin 2, the reserve stock. At the stage of opening bin 2 a new order may be placed. | 1 | 2 |
| Stage 3 | Goods delivered. Bin 1 refilled and sealed, so becoming reserve stock. | 1 | 2 |
| Stage 4 | Procedure begins once more. | | |

It is quite common to have a re-order slip or 'bin tag', which is either attached to the reserve bin or prepared when the re-order level is reached. The tag or slip will be passed to the appropriate department to reorder the item.

A variation frequently used with stationery and printed forms is to insert a re-order slip at an appropriate point within the pack. When this level is reached, the re-ordering process will begin.

## Activity 12 · 5 mins

If you can, identify an item of stock from your workplace that is controlled, or could be controlled by a two-bin system. Suggest a reason why this system is suitable for that stock.

**Session B**

The two-bin system is primarily used for items or materials that are:

- standard;
- relatively low unit value;
- regularly or frequently used;
- readily available from suppliers.

The major advantage of two-bin and similar systems is that cost savings are gained. For one thing, records, such as material requisition notes or job cards, are not usually required. Also, stock control labour costs are generally low.

The two-bin system is simple to operate, provided two key questions are answered correctly.

- What size should the bins be?
- What triggers the reordering process?

If the organization gets these answers wrong, it may have problems with under-stocking or over-stocking.

However, it should be remembered that the vast majority of items stocked at work are not as straightforward as those just described, because:

- they are non-standard items;
- usage varies from time to time;
- supply is not always easy to arrange.

# 4 Managing stock

A typical system for stock control is shown in the following diagram.

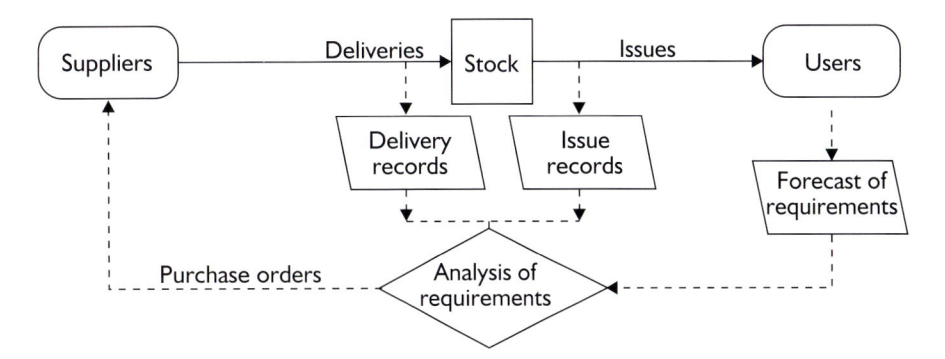

29

**Session B**

You can see that purchase orders are derived from an analysis of requirements, and that the inputs to this are:

- a forecast of what the users think they will need;
- the current stock levels, based on delivery and issue records, and on physical stock checks.

Let's look a little more closely at the way in which stock levels are calculated.

## 4.1 The book stock formula

By knowing the stock level at a certain time (the 'opening stock'), and recording all purchases and issues, we can calculate the stock at a later time (the 'closing stock').

This formula is the **book stock formula**, and is expressed in the following way:

**opening stock + purchases − issues = closing stock**

Here is an example using this formula. If there are 50 reams of paper in stock at the beginning of the month, 100 more are purchased on the 15th of the month and 34 are issued during the month, the closing stock at the end of the month should be as follows.

$$50 + 100 - 34 = 116$$

Assuming the records are accurate, the actual stock level should agree with this figure. This can be physically verified, if required.

**Session B**

## Activity 13

*3 mins*

Complete the following statements.

a At the beginning of the week, 140 disk boxes were in stock. During the week, 120 were delivered by a supplier, and 160 were issued by stores. The closing balance = _____ disk boxes.

b Opening stock + purchases – sales = _____.

c On 1 January, 90 box files were in stock. During the month, 60 were purchased, and at the end of the month 70 were still in stock. _____ files were issued.

d Opening stock + purchases – closing stock = _____.

The answers to this Activity can be found on page 117.

## 4.2 ABC analysis

Because levels of stock are so critical, the stock must be closely managed. Ideally, the organization has to:

- know how much or how many of each item is in stock;
- order goods in advance, to take account of the delay between placing an order and receiving the goods (called the **lead time**);
- ensure that there aren't too many of any item, because that costs money;
- ensure that there aren't too few of any item, because that might impede the organization's business;
- be aware of any deterioration, damage, pilferage or obsolescence, as soon as it occurs;
- ensure that stock is used strictly in rotation.

Again, however, we have to make compromises, because management itself costs money. For large stores, it simply isn't feasible to monitor every item this closely. An organization must find the right balance between the cost of controlling stock and the losses incurred as a result of not controlling it.

## Session B

One way of achieving this balance is to use **ABC analysis**. At its simplest, ABC analysis is a means of categorizing items of stock on the basis of their usage value.

The usage value is calculated in the following way:

**usage value = cost of the item × number issued or sold annually**

Any store, whether in a hospital, a manufacturing firm, a service company or any other type of organization, will have items ranging in usage value.

For example, a DIY store will stock items ranging from very expensive power tools, to middle-range merchandise such as tins of paint, to small packets of screws. These goods will vary in their popularity, as well as their cost and price.

ABC analysis is a modification of the Pareto principle, or the 80:20 rule as it is often known. Pareto was a nineteenth-century Italian philosopher and economist who showed that the bulk of value is likely to be held by a very small proportion of the total items. While Pareto was originally concerned with wealth, his principle was found to occur in so many other situations that the term 80:20 rule was coined. Generally, for example,

**in any store, about 20 per cent of all the items held will account for about 80 per cent of the usage value.**

In other words, the Pareto principle suggests the following:

- 20 per cent of the stock produces 80 per cent of the value of sales or issues.
- 80 per cent of the stock produces 20 per cent of the value of sales or issues.

## Activity 14

*2 mins*

Tick which of the following categories should have the greater attention and give reasons for your choice:

a  the 20 per cent of the stock that produces 80 per cent of the value of sales or issues. ☐

b  the 80 per cent of the stock that produces 20 per cent of the value of sales or issues. ☐

**Session B**

The question was which should have the **greater** attention. Generally, the items in category (a) would be given more consideration because the relatively small number of them produce a far greater proportion of the income. The absence of one item in this category could well have a serious effect on production or customers. However, the items in category (b) may also be important. For example, the effect of running out of invoice forms might be very inconvenient.

The conclusion must be that all items require an effective stock-control system, but that for some the system need not be so complex or costly.

In the DIY store, high-priced power tools may not sell in large quantities, but they are likely to represent a fairly high percentage of total sales. It therefore makes sense to spend more money on accounting for these items, and protecting them from would-be shoplifters, than (say) counting the number of nails in stock. This is not to say that the nails are not worth stocking; instead, it means that the loss of a few nails won't be a great financial loss.

## Activity 15

*3 mins*

To take another example, suppose an office supply company sells 4000 pencils a year costing 55 pence, and sells 150 photocopiers each costing £650. Which has the greater usage value?

The answer is as follows.

cost of pencil × annual sales = usage value
£0.55 × 4000 = £2200

cost of photocopier × annual sales = usage value
£650 × 150 = £97,500

You can see that the photocopier has much greater usage value, even though its annual sales are quite modest.

**Session B**

When the Pareto principle is applied to stock management, we usually adopt three categories, A, B and C, rather than the two categories of 80:20.

- Category A items are those small in number, but high in usage value. They are critical from the financial viewpoint.
- Category B items are medium in both number and usage value.
- Category C items are high in number, but have low usage value.

In a typical workplace, the percentage of items in each of the categories A, B, and C might be as follows.

| Category | Approximate % of total items | % of usage value | Comment |
|---|---|---|---|
| A | 10 | 75–85 | High usage value, small number – critical: close control. |
| B | 10–30 | 10–20 | Medium number and usage value: medium to close control. |
| C | 50–60 | 5–10 | High number of items, low usage value: less frequent control. |

**Session B**

## Activity 16

*6 mins*

In your workplace, try to identify **three** stock items: one of high cost value and low quantity issues or sales; one of medium cost and quantity; one of low cost and high quantity use. Calculate their usage values.

Item 1 (high cost, low quantity)


Item 2 (medium cost and quantity)


Item 3 (low cost, high quantity)


You may have chosen three items close in usage value, but it's more likely that the high cost, low quantity item had the highest usage value, followed by the medium cost, medium quantity item.

ABC analysis consists of the following steps.

1   Calculate the usage value for each item.

2   Rank the items in order of usage value, with the most valuable item at the top.

3   Find the total usage value of all items. Express each item's usage value as a percentage of the total usage value.

4   Calculate the cumulative percentages, working from the top.

5   Classify each item into A, B and C categories by percentage. There is no hard and fast rule for setting boundaries between categories, and this will be a management decision.

**Session B**

The following is a small example, showing how a list of items stocked by a furniture company worked out.

| Item | Cost (£) | Annual sales (£) | Usage value (£) | Category |
|---|---|---|---|---|
| Wall unit | 300 | 1,100 | 330,000 | A |
| Armchair | 125 | 2,300 | 287,500 | A |
| Shelving unit | 75 | 2,000 | 150,000 | A |
| Table | 124 | 1,200 | 148,800 | A |
| Chair | 45 | 3,000 | 135,000 | A |
| Bench | 155 | 650 | 100,750 | B |
| Sofa | 173 | 450 | 77,850 | B |
| Cabinet | 108 | 560 | 60,480 | B |
| Chest | 230 | 220 | 50,600 | B |
| Telephone table | 35 | 400 | 14,000 | C |
| Carpet rod | 2 | 5,000 | 10,000 | C |
| Window frame | 35 | 200 | 7,000 | C |
| Kit of parts | 15 | 450 | 6,750 | C |
| Wall bracket | 22 | 250 | 5,500 | C |
| Shelf A | 18 | 300 | 5,400 | C |
| Shelf B | 17 | 300 | 5,100 | C |
| Hanger | 1 | 1,200 | 1,200 | C |
| Bracket | 5 | 200 | 1,000 | C |
| Holder | 4 | 250 | 1,000 | C |
| Arm | 2 | 300 | 600 | C |

In this case, it was decided to place the items realizing around 75 per cent of the total usage value into category A, another 20 per cent or so in category B, and the rest in category C.

**Session B**

ABC analysis should assist in identifying the amount and nature of attention that individual items require.

Now, we'll move on to discuss two major aspects of storekeeping: receiving and issuing goods, together with the documentation associated with these activities.

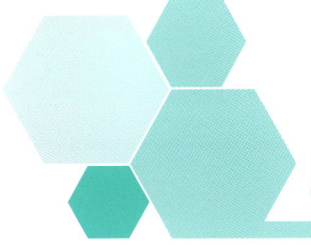

# 5 Receiving goods

What happens when goods are received into stores?

## 5.1 Essential steps

Whatever industry you work in, the essential steps of receiving goods remain the same.

### Activity 17 · 3 mins

Assume that you work in your organization's stores. Suppose a lorry arrives at the door, and you are told by the driver that he or she has brought some materials for you. What would be the first few things you would do?

# Session B

> EXTENSION 2
> Section 7 of the international standard on *Quality Management Systems*, ISO 9001, has a good deal to say about various aspects of stock control, such as verifying materials purchased and maintaining good documentation.

Before they are unloaded, you should check the following:

- that the goods really are for your organization, and that they have arrived at the right entrance or delivery point;
- whether the goods have some hazard associated with them – such materials should be clearly marked, and you may need to arrange for special equipment;
- what is to be done with the materials: they may be urgently required by someone, or they may be routine items to be placed into stores;
- the best way to unload the vehicle, while bearing in mind the safety of personnel, and the availability of appropriate unloading gear;
- that an area is available for the goods to be placed.

Following these preliminary checks, the goods receiving function will typically need to:

- supervise the unloading of the goods, and their transfer to the correct area;
- check quantities;
- check that the goods appear to be in satisfactory condition;
- check to see that the supplier's documentation is correct, and to record the transaction according to the organization's procedures;
- arrange for the materials to be inspected.

## 5.2 Documentation

Most organizations these days have computerized stores systems and we will look at developments in this area at the end of the section. However, it would be useful to look first in some detail at two documents that are normally used in a manual system. This should help you to appreciate many aspects of stores documentation.

There are two possible transactions involved in the receipt of goods:

- taking in new goods, just delivered by a supplier;
- taking back old goods, which had been issued and which are now being returned for some reason.

For stores records purposes it is essential that these two transactions do not get confused. In both cases a record must be made of the transaction.

- **New** goods need to be checked against orders by stores personnel and in many organizations they will need to be notified to the people responsible for purchasing and accounting, so that they can be paid for. A **goods received note (GRN)** is usually completed.

**Session B**

- **Returns** have already been booked into the stores, paid for and booked out again; however, they still have to be recorded. A **goods returned note** (or debit note) is the document used in this case.

The information that appears on these documents must be sufficient for everybody concerned to understand the full details of transaction.

Although each company will have its own particular design for its goods received notes and goods returned notes, there are a number of pieces of information that must always be shown.

### The goods received note (GRN)

These obviously vary from one organization to another but all contain basically the same information.

## Activity 18

3 mins

Jot down **four** pieces of information you think it is important should appear on a goods received note so that each department can get the information it needs.

___

___

___

___

The words 'Goods Received Note' should appear in a prominent position, accompanied by the following.

- A serial number

    This identifies each goods received note (GRN), and distinguishes it from every other GRN.

- The date of the receipt

    Making sure the correct date is on every document helps when tracing materials; sometimes, the time of the receipt is also noted.

39

**Session B**

- For each item received:

  - the quantity should be recorded – if a delivery is made up of more than one item, each part of the delivery must be checked separately and shortages and surpluses must be noted;

  - the description should be given – the description helps to identify the goods; even when a code is used, a description is used to act as a confirmation;

  - a code number or reference number – in many workplaces, codes are used, to avoid confusion caused by vague or incomplete descriptions. In a code such as 'TRP05/KP/FS': 'TRP05' might refer to the product ('typist's office chair type 5'); 'KP' to the supplier ('Kent Plastics'), and 'FS' may indicate that the goods are to be stored in the 'furniture and stationery stores'.

- The order number relating to the delivery

  Sometimes an order is delivered in several batches, perhaps over a number of days or even weeks. The order number is used to match each goods received note with the original order.

- The name of the supplier

  In case of queries, damaged goods, and so on, the supplier will need to be contacted.

- The signature of the person who checks the delivery

  Normally, only authorized people should be allowed to check in goods.

  In addition, there may also be spaces for other items such as:

- the method of delivery (e.g. rail, van, post, courier);
- the name of the organization delivering the goods;
- the exact time of the delivery;
- the condition of goods when received.

  Here is an example of a goods received note that you might like to compare with whatever is used in your workplace.

**Session B**

| Toys For You Ltd. Tiny Works | | GOODS RECEIVED NOTE | |
|---|---|---|---|
| Supplier | Date | Serial No. | |
| | Carrier | Order No. | |
| Quantity | Description | Reference No. | |
| | | | |
| For office use | | Counted and checked by: | |
| Ledger No. | Bin No. | | |

## Activity 19

*2 mins*

Which people or departments in an organization are likely to need a copy of a goods received note?

_____

_____

_____

_____

The way things are done in your own organization will depend on its size and the way it is run. In a typical large organization:

- one copy is kept by the stores;
- one copy is sent to the purchasing department, so they know that the supplier has delivered the goods ordered;
- one copy is sent to the accounts department, so that payment can be arranged.

Sometimes a copy will be given to the department wanting the goods, to let them know they have arrived.

41

**Session B**

## The goods returned note

All internal departments sending goods back to the stores would need to complete a goods returned note which stores can match up to the original documentation.

If the goods are being returned from outside the organization then stores will need to complete a goods returned note that can be matched up to the original sales order and to any other documentation relating to the return. This might include, for instance, a note from the salesman authorizing the return.

### Activity 20

*2 mins*

Suggest **two** items of information that should appear on a goods returned note, which do not appear on a goods received note.

_____

_____

As well as a serial number, description of the items returned, and how many were received, there would normally be:

- the reason for the return;
- the department or customer returning the goods;
- the job number (or other reference) for which the goods were originally issued;
- the signature of the manager of the department that returned the goods.

On page 43 is an example of a typical goods returned note.

Copies of the goods returned note may be required by:

- the stores, for re-adjusting the record of what is in stock;
- the person or department who returned the goods;
- the costing department, so that any cross-department charges may be made;
- the appropriate department who produced the goods originally.

Copies are often colour-coded, to help ensure that each department gets the correct copy.

**Session B**

| Toys For You Ltd. Tiny Works | | GOODS RETURNED TO STORE No. | |
|---|---|---|---|
| From Department | Date returned | GRN Reference | |
| | Date of issue | | |
| Job No. | Supplier | | Order No. |
| Quantity | Description | | Reference No. |
| | | | |
| Reason for return | | Authorizing signature | |
| For office use | | Counted and checked by: | |
| Ledger No. | Bin No. | | |

## 6 Issuing goods

If you are responsible for a stores function, you will appreciate the importance of providing a first-class service in the issue of materials. This is the most visible aspect of stores work, and it is often the activity by which others in the organization will judge you.

Again, it is helpful to look at the documentation procedures.

As with receiving deliveries, two types of transaction may be involved in the issuing of goods:

- providing a person, customer or department with the goods they request from stores;
- returning goods to a supplier, because they are faulty, damaged or unsuitable.

Typically, the corresponding documents are:

- a **customer order**, or internal **materials requisition**;
- a **credit note** and **returns note**.

**Session B**

## 6.1 Materials requisition

Once again, these materials vary in detail between organizations but the key information remains the same.

### Activity 21 · 3 mins

Jot down **five** items of information that you think should appear on a materials requisition form.

_____
_____
_____
_____
_____

One version of a materials requisition form is shown below.

| *Toys For You Ltd.* *Tiny Works* | | MATERIALS REQUISITION | |
|---|---|---|---|
| | | Serial No. | |
| From Department | Date requested | | Date required |
| Required for job: | Supplier (if known) | | |
| Quantity | Description | | Code |
| | | | |
| For office use | | Authorizing signature | |

44

**Session B**

Key items are the:

- serial number – to identify each individual requisition;
- date;
- quantity of each item;
- description of each item;
- code or reference number;
- job or batch number for which the goods are required;
- name of the department making the requisition;
- signature of the supervisor or manager of the department making the requisition.

As with goods received documents, three copies are typically required: the person or department making the requisition needs a copy; as does the stores; and the department whose job it is to cost work also needs a copy.

## 6.2 Goods returned to supplier

For goods returned to the supplier, we have another document, also sometimes called a 'goods returned note'. This can be confusing, as we can't tell from the name whether the goods are being returned to stores, or to the supplier. We'll call it a **returns to supplier note**.

### Activity 22  *3 mins*

Now list **five** items of information that you would include on a returns to supplier note.

_____
_____
_____
_____
_____

45

**Session B**

A returns to supplier note should match up with the original order, GRN, and materials requisition. It would usually include:

- a serial number unique to that particular document;
- date of the return;
- quantity of each item returned;
- description of the items returned;
- code or reference number for each type of item returned;
- reason for the return;
- date of the original delivery;
- name of supplier;
- serial number of the goods received note;
- original order number;
- signature of the person authorizing the return.

You might also have included the method of return (post, rail, road transport, etc.) and the name of the company carrying the returned goods.

## 7 Stock levels

As mentioned earlier, it is a basic rule of stock control that we should keep the minimum amount of stocks that are necessary for uninterrupted operation. This saves money, space and work, and reduces shrinkage.

The **minimum stock** is the lowest possible level you should hold to avoid any danger of running out.

It is not the same as the re-order level: it is lower. Sometimes, a **safety stock** level is set slightly below the minimum stock level. The organization will aim to re-order so that the stock issued during the lead time, while awaiting delivery, does not eat into the safety stock.

**Session B**

## Activity 23

*3 mins*

Here is a diagram of a theoretical stock level record, as it is affected by issues and lead times.

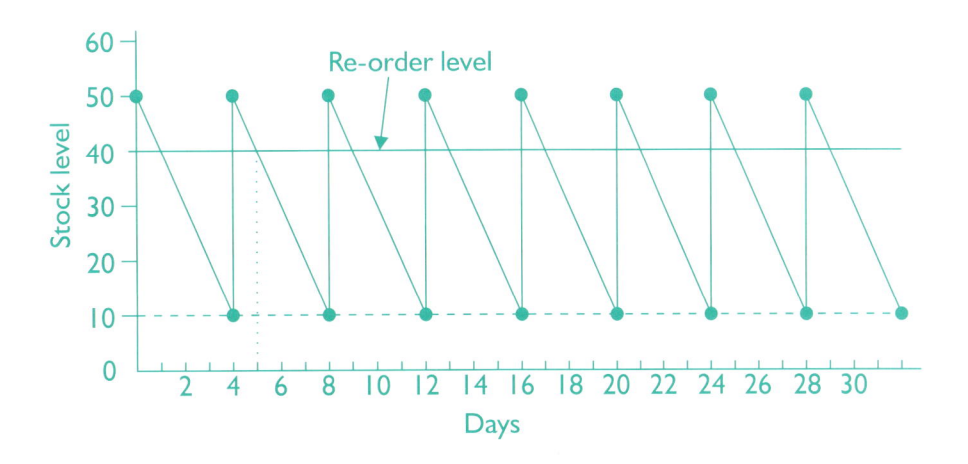

According to this diagram answer the following questions.

- What is the lead time for deliveries? _____

- What is the order quantity? _____

- What is the minimum stock level? _____

This is a very regular pattern – rather unrealistic, in reality – in which the re-order point is a stock level of 40, the lead time for delivery is three days, the order quantity is 40, and the minimum stock level (and in practice, the safety stock) is 10.

In the real world, the rate of use of the stock would vary, so that stock levels would sometimes rise above 40, and the re-order quantity might have to be changed on occasions. Sometimes it would be necessary to use part of the minimum stock. The point of having a safety or minimum stock is that it **can** be used: it is there for use in an emergency. A more realistic diagram is shown on page 48.

**Session B**

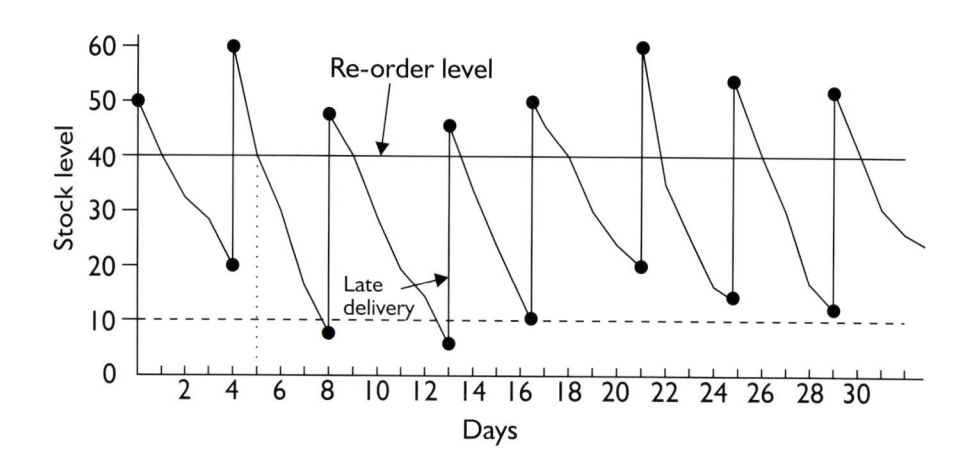

Here, levels are recorded daily, and the delivery period of three days is assumed to start exactly at the time the level reaches 40. You can see that one delivery was late, taking four days instead of three.

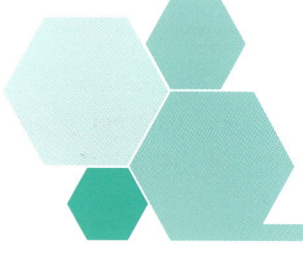

# 8 Computerized systems

## 8.1 Computerized receipt of goods

It is usual for goods received notes, goods returned notes and other documents to be generated by a computerized system, and automatically distributed to the various departments, perhaps via e-mail.

In a computerized stores system, the following actions typically take place on receipt of goods into stores.

1 At the point where the goods are received, an operator keys in data giving details of the items.

2 The computer will check to see that this information is valid and appropriate, and, so far as it is possible to tell, that the operator has not made any mistakes.

3 If special actions are necessary, such as inspection or certification, the computer will advise the operator of this fact. It may also pass on this information to others who need to know, by sending messages to their computer terminals.

4 The computer stock records for each item will be adjusted automatically.

**Session B**

5   A goods received note will be generated by the computer, and copies printed out in the areas where they are required. This may not take the form that we have looked at, but may instead be printed or displayed as a summary report of all items received during a certain period.

A very modern system may be even more automated, and involve little, if any, keying in of data or paper printouts. We'll explain this in more detail when we come to the topic of Supply Chain Management in Session C.

## 8.2 Computerized issue of goods

If the stores system is computerized the person requiring goods will be able to select them from a menu and enter quantities and other specifications as appropriate. This 'electronic requisition' can then be sent to the stores area, just like an internal e-mail.

In the stores area, the message will be automatically processed and relevant information, such as the warehouse location of the item(s) ordered, will also be shown. Orders might be consolidated so that, if three different people have ordered the same item, stores personnel can collect all the orders in one visit rather than wearing their legs out with three visits!

Some systems can devise an optimum 'picking route'. Picking is the name given to the process of extracting ordered goods from their locations in stores: it's a bit like picking the ripe fruit from the trees in an orchard.

### Activity 24 · 5 mins

On page 50 is an illustration showing an extract from a fictional organization's computerized stock requisition system. How could the system be improved?

49

**Session B**

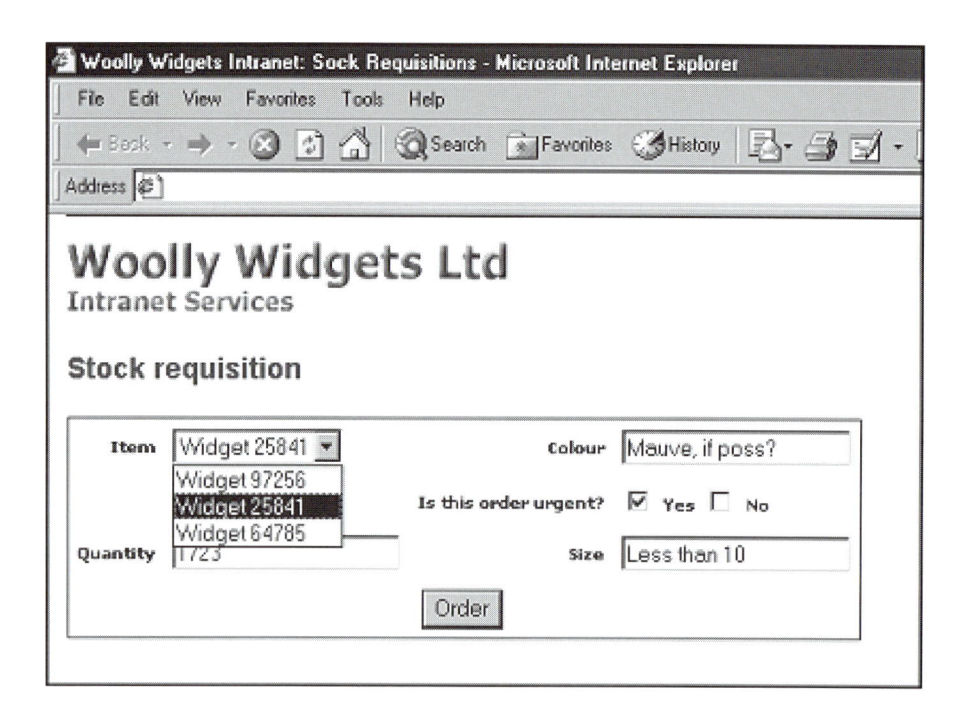

This requisition will probably have to be sent back to the user for clarification, or else the user will receive the wrong part on the wrong date.

- One problem is that users can enter any information they like in the Colour and Size fields. Presumably Widgets are only available in a specific range of colours and specific sizes: the form should therefore offer the user only the options that are actually available.
- The other problem is the Yes/No choice: most people will choose Yes whether or not their need for the item is particularly urgent. It would be much better to force the user to enter a specific date.

You may have identified additional problems, including the title of the screen.

## 8.3 The use of robots in materials handling

Robots have been employed in industry for a number of years. By 'robot', we mean a machine capable of carrying out a complex series of actions automatically. Robots are especially useful where repetitive but precise movements need to be made.

One example of a robot is the **automated guided vehicle (AGV)**. This is typically employed in moving heavy or palleted goods around a warehouse.

**Session B**

There are a number of guidance systems for AGVs. They may follow the path of:

- wires laid beneath the floor – these wires create a magnetic field that is detected by the steering system of the AGV;
- painted white lines on the floor, the AGV detecting the position of these using light sensors;
- infra-red or visible beams, which are again detected with appropriate sensors.

Alternatively, the AGV may be free-ranging, and kept under control via a computer that sends radio signals.

## Activity 25 · 3 mins

Suggest **two** or more advantages of using robots such as AGVs in materials handling.

_____
_____
_____
_____
_____
_____
_____
_____

Robots such as AGVs hold several advantages where the initial expense can be justified.

- Robots are able to work for longer periods of time than can people, without becoming tired or bored.
- Work is generally done more consistently, and faster, than by humans.
- Their ability to operate with precision usually results in fewer incidents of damage.
- Robots often improve an organization's health and safety record, as there are fewer humans doing awkward jobs or lifting heavy weights.

**Session B**

## 8.4 Bar coding

You will no doubt be familiar with the bar code system used to identify and price many types of goods sold in supermarkets and other retail outlets. These consist of a series of dark bars, separated by spaces, as shown in this example.

The bars are read by a device that sends a beam of light onto the bar code panel, and detects their reflections, or by a 'light pen' that must be passed across the bar code.

Bar coding is also employed in many industrial applications, for item identification. There are several types of coding in use.

The main benefits that may be gained from using a bar code system include:

- the speed of recording information;
- and the level of detail which may be encoded.

## 8.5 Warehouse management systems

Very modern organizations use a combination of all the technologies above and others, most notably Radio Frequency (RF) systems. An RF system uses portable terminals that have a built in bar code scanner, a small screen and a keyboard. These are either carried by staff or mounted on vehicles or robots. They are connected via a radio link to the main computer system, including the accounting system and any production systems.

A fully-fledged warehouse management system has many advantages. Although it will be expensive to install it can offer considerable savings.

- Information about materials movements should be far less prone to error.
- It is much easier and quicker to locate any item held in the warehouse.
- Stock levels are updated instantly and perfectly accurately.
- Orders for new stocks will be placed automatically when needed.

**Session B**

# Self-assessment 2

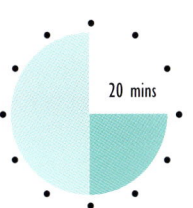

20 mins

1  Explain what is meant by the statement: 'Stock is a buffer between supply and demand.'

   _____
   _____
   _____
   _____
   _____

2  The following diagram was used to explain the two-bin system, but the words have been removed. Write an explanation in your own words in the boxes on the left.

| | | |
|---|---|---|
| Stage 1 | 1 (main) | 2 (reserve) |
| Stage 2 | 1 | 2 |
| Stage 3 | 1 | 2 |
| Stage 4 | | |

53

## Session B

3   Work out the usage value of the following items:

| Item | Unit cost (£) | Annual sales | Usage value(£) |
|---|---|---|---|
| Vacuum cleaner | 230 | 500 | |
| Microwave oven | 340 | 750 | |
| Refrigerator | 175 | 330 | |
| Installing kit | 25 | 1000 | |
| Spares kit | 45 | 120 | |

4   Summarize the principles behind ABC analysis, in your own words.

_____

_____

_____

_____

_____

5   Fill in the blanks in the following sentences with suitable words, chosen from the list underneath.

   a   Stock is a _____ between supply and _____, or between the suppliers and the users.

   b   Organizations generally aim to keep the _____ stocks in the minimum _____ for the minimum time.

   c   Having stocks too _____ is bad news; having stocks too _____ may be worse news.

   d   Opening stock + _____ – issues = closing stock.

   e   In any store, about _____ of all the items held will account for about _____ of the usage value.

   | 20 PER CENT | 80 PER CENT | BUFFER |
   | DEMAND | HIGH | LOW |
   | MINIMUM | PURCHASES | SPACE |

6   a   What documentation is required when receiving goods? Why do the purchasing and accounts departments need a copy?
    b   What are the minimum stock level and safety stock level?

Answers to these questions can be found on pages 114–15.

## 8 Summary

- Stock is a buffer between supply and demand, or between the suppliers and the users.

- There are many costs entailed in holding stocks, and the general aim is to keep the minimum stocks in the minimum space for the minimum time. However, it can be more costly, and more detrimental to the organization's objectives, if stocks are too low.

- To help reduce shrinkage, stock rotation is used. One simple example is the two-bin system.

- The book stock formula is expressed in the following way:

    opening stock + purchases − issues = closing stock

- ABC analysis is a method of determining the relative amount of attention that should be given to goods in stock. A usage value is calculated for each item, which is the purchase price times the number issued or sold; the highest usage value items then receive the greatest amount of attention.

- Typical items of documentation for receiving goods are the goods received note (GRN), and the goods returned note. For issuing of stocks, the corresponding documents are the customer order or materials requisition, and the returns to supplier note.

- The minimum stock is the lowest possible level you should hold to avoid any danger of running out.

- Where materials management is computerized, the above documents may be issued in the form of a summary report, and automatically routed to the sections that need them.

- The computerized issue of goods can control and consolidate rquirements so that stock can be issued with the maximum efficiency.

- The use of technology in materials management also includes robots, bar coding and radio frequency systems.

# Session C
# Purchasing, resource planning and security

## 1 Introduction

This last session deals with four aspects of materials resource management.

- **The purchasing function**

    The job of purchasing is to obtain the right materials and other items, of the right specification and quality, from the right source, in the right quantity, at the right time and place, and at the right price.

    As such, it is a key function in the organization's management of resources.

    We look at some uses of technology that are commonly used to assist the purchasing function: Electronic Date Interchange (EDI), e-procurement and business exchanges.

- **Materials planning**

    We look at two powerful techniques here: just-in-time, and materials requirements planning (MRP).

- **Resource planning and management**

    Computerized methods of resource planning are increasingly practical for many businesses as computing costs reduce because bespoke solutions are no longer always necessary. We consider three software-based tools: Manufacturing Resource Planning, Enterprise Resource Planning and Supply Chain Management.

**Session C**

- Security

One of the main concerns of resource managers is the security of expensive materials and equipment. Our brief review of this subject is intended to help you apply the principles of good security.

Although these four topics may seem to be unrelated, our discussions of them should help us to tie together some of the themes covered earlier in this workbook.

## 2 The purchasing function

Let's just remind ourselves of the diagram for stock control, and how the purchasing function fits into the general scheme of things.

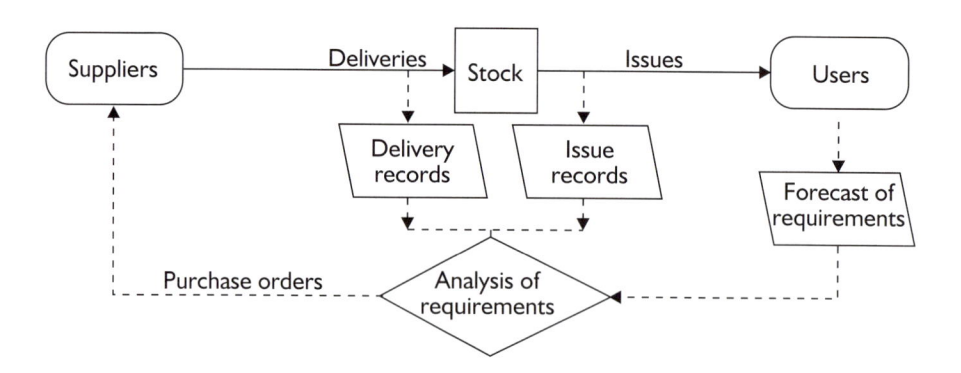

Purchase orders are sent to suppliers as a result of an analysis of requirements. This may happen when:

- new goods are needed by the users;
- the re-order level for existing goods is reached.

The existing level may be determined by visually inspecting the stock, but is more often calculated from the records of deliveries and issues.

**Session C**

## 2.1 The purchasing function

Typical day-to-day purchasing for an individual might involve a quick trip to the local corner shop to buy essentials.

Organizational purchasing (sometimes called '**procurement**') is more like the process you would go through to get the same essentials when you are in a strange town: you'd have to find out where the nearest shop is, find out how to get there, work out the shelf layout, queue for a certain length of time. The process may continue on other days, when you discover that another shop offers lower prices and is quicker to serve you.

Organizational purchasing involves the following activities.

- Finding suitable suppliers

  When a new item is needed, a reliable supplier must be found. Staff who are regularly involved in purchasing will have regular contact with suppliers' representatives, and will usually be able to locate two or three potential vendors fairly quickly.

- Minimizing the cost of purchases

  Invariably, there will be differences in prices between suppliers, for any particular item. It is therefore important that the user or designer provides the purchasing officer with a specification of the goods, including perhaps dimensions, finish, colour, type and so on. Comparisons between suppliers' offerings can then be made on the basis of 'Which product will meet our requirements at minimum overall cost?' Quantity will obviously affect cost, as most suppliers will be willing to give discounts for bulk purchases. The purchasing function has the task of obtaining goods and services on the most favourable terms. Competitive tenders may be invited from contractors for larger value goods.

- Arranging for goods to be delivered when and where they are needed

  Just as important as cost is delivery to 'the right time and the right place'. It is a fact of life that suppliers will sometimes give false information in order to obtain a contract. Experienced purchasing personnel will be wary of promises of delivery dates by unknown or unreliable suppliers.

- Maintaining good relations with suppliers and with other parts of the organization

  Purchasing acts as a link between suppliers and users. Its main task is to provide a service for the rest of the organization, not only in obtaining the required goods, but in giving appropriate advice and information.

**Session C**

Where large quantities are being bought, and the buying organization is spending large sums of money, the supplier–purchaser relationship has to be managed carefully. It is obviously in the interests of both parties to find ways around any problems that may arise, and the purchasing officer plays a crucial role in these negotiations.

## Activity 26 · 3 mins

From the above, what would you say were the benefits to the organization of a well-managed purchasing function? Try to list at least **three** benefits.

_____
_____
_____
_____
_____
_____

If the purchasing function is well handled, the organization should benefit from:

- cost savings, through obtaining goods at lower prices;
- assured supplies;
- lower inventory costs, as a result of having materials at the place and time they're needed;
- good supplier relationships;
- reduced lead times;
- reduced materials obsolescence;
- improved quality control.

## 2.2 Electronic Data Interchange (EDI)

**Electronic Data Interchange (EDI)** is the electronic exchange of business documents (purchase orders, invoices, application forms, etc.) from one organization's computer to another organization's computer in standard data formats.

EDI emerged in the **late 1960s** when many industry groups realised that processing the large volume of paper documentation accompanying the shipment of goods resulted in significant delays in settlement and product deliveries.

It is currently estimated that **around 175,000 companies** all over the world (consisting primarily of very large public companies and their numerous trading partners) conduct business using EDI. The list of industries in which EDI is actively used includes shipping, retail, grocery, clothing and textiles, financial, health care and many others. There are three main components of an EDI system (in addition to each organization's own applications, for instance its own accounting system).

- **EDI standards**

    EDI standards eliminate the need for human intervention in the interpretation of incoming and outgoing data. EDI is based on a set of standard formats that define 'transaction sets', which can be used to send basic business data from one computer to another.

    These transaction sets replace paper documents such as purchase orders, invoices, and so on. Standards define the structure, format, and content of EDI documents, including the data fields that may be included in a document, and the sequence and format of fields.

- **EDI gateway**

    An EDI gateway reformats outgoing data from an organisation-specific format into an EDI standard format and adds data that enables the EDI message to be routed properly to a trading partner.

- **A communication network**

    The main methods of actually communicating the message are through a direct connection, via a Value Added Network Service (VANS) – which is not unlike the Internet except that access is restricted to specific organizations, such as travel agents and airlines – or, in more recent years, via the Internet.

**Session C**

## Activity 27

*4 mins*

We said that EDI standards 'eliminate the need for human intervention in the interpretation of incoming and outgoing data'. What do you think this means and why is it a good thing?

_____

_____

_____

_____

EDI has advantages for the organization ordering goods and for the organisation supplying them.

- The ordering organization enters the details of the order, perhaps using an online catalogue and picking from menu options to save time and avoid errors. The order does not have to be printed out and posted: it is sent via telecommunications and arrives at the supplier's offices almost instantaneously.

- The supplying organisation does not have to transcribe a paper order onto its own computer systems, again, saving a large amount of time and eliminating transcription errors. The incoming EDI order automatically updates the stock system and the accounting ledgers.

## 2.3 EDI on the Internet

Ever since EDI was first introduced, large companies have always wanted their smaller suppliers to use EDI. But it was far too expensive.

- Implementing EDI meant purchasing and integrating an unusual combination of software, hardware, and services with an initial cost that could exceed £70,000.
- Transporting data using private or industry-specific Value Added Network Services (VANS) could cost upward of £15,000 per year.

Trading partners of large companies have faced a tough choice until recently: they could either pay the going price of EDI or lose their large company customer.

**Session C**

Web-based EDI services now present the opportunity for everyone to enjoy the undoubted benefits of EDI services.

- EDI on the Internet costs less to buy – prices range from free to about £350 per month, depending on usage. For instance, subscribers to IBM's Web-based service pay as little as £25 per month for a subset of EDI services that once cost between 10 to 100 times as much.

- EDI on the Internet is open and accessible. It is available wherever the Internet is available.

There are, nevertheless, some issues still to be addressed. In particular many companies have substantial investments in their bought-and-paid-for EDI systems and in integrating them with back-end applications. They do not want to retire their systems prematurely, nor do they wish to end up supporting two systems that essentially do the same thing.

## 2.4 E-procurement or B2B

Many of us have bought a product over the Internet – a book from Amazon, say, or the week's groceries from Tesco.com.

Organizations can do this too, of course: the process is called '**e-procurement**' or '**B2B**' (business-to-business) and it is now very widely used for non-production purchases such as office supplies.

One-off organizational purchases may be made online in exactly the same way as an individual would make them, using an organizational credit card.

If online purchases are made regularly it is more likely that the organization will have an account with the supplier. An authorised and registered user will log in using a password and the organization will periodically be billed by the supplier. Depending on the status of the buying organization there may be discounts for volume purchasing or other special offers.

The supplying organization can set up its website so that it recognizes the purchaser once logged in and presents a list of 'favourites', i.e. items that the purchaser regularly buys. This saves searching for the items required and also avoids the need to key in name, address and delivery details.

B2B offers similar advantages to EDI in terms of speed and elimination of unnecessary work. It also offers the purchasing organization much wider choice than it might have had otherwise. In theory, resources can be sourced from suppliers anywhere in the world, perhaps at much lower prices than could be obtained if the organization only considered local suppliers.

**Session C**

For items where speed or cost of delivery is an issue it may not always be practical to order from a supplier in, for example, China, but a London firm, may find it gets better value if it orders from a supplier in Manchester rather than the local supplier it had used previously.

## Activity 28

*3 mins*

Can you see any potential problems for an organisation that allows its purchasing department to use e-procurement?

___

___

___

___

The main issue is control: if anyone can order goods from anywhere there is a major risk that unauthorised purchases will be made. There is also an increased likelihood that purchases will be made from suppliers who cannot deliver the required quality (or cannot deliver at all!). For this reason, companies such as Ariba have developed special e-procurement software with built-in tools to control who can place orders at various spending levels, who orders should be placed with and so on.

## 2.5 Business exchanges

Following on from the success of e-procurement, organizations in many industries are now developing **business exchanges**. Typically an exchange gathers together the major enterprises in a given market sector – let's say, car manufacturing and creates a market-place of sufficient volume to attract increased numbers of suppliers.

All the participants in the formation of the exchange will ask their existing suppliers to join in, thus creating the beginnings of a supplier pool. If each participant adds their own existing suppliers then all participants will immediately be able to enjoy the benefits of increased choice and competition.

A notable example is Covisint, which brings together all the major motor manufacturers – Ford, General Motors, Nissan, Renault and so on.

**Session C**

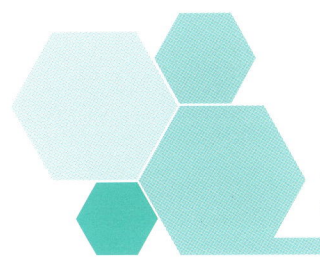

# 3 Materials planning

For any sizeable organization, the problems of stock control and planning are considerable.

As we have seen, stock is a buffer between supply and demand; it may also be a considerable drain on the organization's finances.

One approach is to do without stocks altogether.

## 3.1 Less than the minimum: 'just-in-time'

A very large organization has considerable power over its suppliers, who can seldom afford to lose its custom. Knowing this, the organization with the huge buying power may, in effect, make the following statement to its suppliers:

EXTENSION 3
The radical approach to production is examined in David Hitchins' book.

**'Sorry, we're no longer prepared to go to the trouble and expense of storing your products. From now on that's your problem.'**

- Supermarket retailers try not to hold stocks except on the sales floor; if they have a stockroom, it is purely a transit point where goods-in are received and checked before being put out on to the shelves.

  Retailers will always say 'if the customers can't see it, it isn't selling', so it makes complete commercial sense to avoid holding stocks in a back room somewhere. The rule for retail stock ordering is 'little and often'.

- Large manufacturing and assembly firms also try to do without having large stocks of components. They arrange for parts and materials to be delivered at exactly the time when they are needed, to be fed directly into the assembly lines.

  These are called **just-in-time** (JIT) systems. The whole operation has to be highly organized to keep these large-scale enterprises fully stocked and running smoothly at all times.

**Session C**

## Activity 29

*3 mins*

Write down **two** ways in which the JIT system differs from the traditional type of stores supply operation.

---

Perhaps the points you identified are among the following. Just-in-time systems depend on:

- frequent and relatively small deliveries;
- very short lead times;
- close communication between the user and the supplier.

It may also have occurred to you that supermarkets that use just-in-time will also need:

- frequent, perhaps continuous, stock checks;
- computers to record the movement of goods in and out and to calculate the orders required;
- high-speed communication systems to transmit orders instantly to the suppliers.

Manufacturers that use just-in-time may depend on being able to:

- plan and forecast production rates;
- agree requirements in advance with their suppliers.

When the suppliers themselves need time to manufacture or assemble their products, advance planning is essential. The supplier and the user also need to communicate frequently in order to adjust and confirm the precise timing and volume of deliveries.

This is not possible without the aid of sophisticated technology, as the following real-life case history shows.

## Session C

A major car company, in its factory in the North East, has installed a system whereby a special coding tag on a car being built triggers a message to a supplier of carpets, boot linings and parcel shelves. There are 120 possible variations for these components, depending on colour, engine size, extras and whether the model is left-hand or right-hand drive. The component supplier has a factory just two miles away, and it makes deliveries up to 60 times a day.

When the message is received by computer link, machines and operators at the supplier select, trim and fit plastic extras, before stacking them in sequence and loading them on trucks in small batches. On arrival, the driver takes the stock straight to the assembly line.

The car manufacturer's management say that the system brings 100 per cent savings on inventory, 100 per cent savings on internal handling, and 90 per cent to 95 per cent savings on space, as well as productivity advantages. The dangers inherent in the system are also recognized. As the supplier's managing director says, 'If we failed to supply a part immediately it would shut down the plant.'

## Activity 30

*3 mins*

On the whole, just-in-time has been used only by large-scale businesses. Try to suggest **two** reasons why this is so.

_____

_____

Just-in-time is very inconvenient for suppliers, who are used to a world in which most of their customers (perhaps including your organization) are content to go along with the traditional way of doing things. This includes:

- delivery during normal hours;
- longish lead times;
- grouped deliveries, perhaps covering several customers in an area;
- largish order quantities, because of the long lead times;
- buying and storing substantial stocks well in advance of when they are actually needed.

**Session C**

Large-scale just-in-time users have the power to insist on suppliers doing what suits **them**, such as:

- delivery at any time of night or day;
- frequent deliveries with very short lead times;
- direct deliveries to them alone;
- relatively small orders at a time.

In practice, vendors need to be located very close, geographically, to the organization they are supplying to.

However, it isn't only large manufacturing corporations that can benefit from the concepts behind JIT. In the past few years, some small and medium-sized hospitals have adopted a policy of having 'stockless inventory systems'. This involves moving some of the supply problems to the suppliers, and eliminating stock from the central storeroom. This brings benefits of reduced costs, but obviously needs careful management and reliable suppliers.

## 3.2 Materials requirements planning

In manufacturing companies, and in some service organizations, the concept of materials requirements planning (MRP) can provide a framework by which scheduling and inventory decisions are made.

MRP is:

- mainly concerned with the scheduling of activities, and the management of stock;
- most useful where components and sub-assemblies are produced, for incorporation in the final product or service.

Here are two examples of organizations that might benefit from applying MRP.

- A computer manufacturing company that assembles PC boards and buys in cabinets, which are brought together in the final product.
- A hotel, which provides not only accommodation but food, a bar service, dry cleaning and so on, in the packages it provides its guests.

In both these cases, the final product to the customer is **dependent** on the provision of lower-level goods or services.

If the number of customers is known or can be estimated, then the organization knows how many of each component must be manufactured, prepared or obtained. So one of the main inputs to the MRP process is a

# Session C

forecast demand. Its outputs are a detailed schedule of all the items that will be required, in order to make up the final product.

EXTENSION 4
If you would like to learn more about MRP, the book listed in this extension is a useful source of information.

The other inputs are the **bill of requirements** (or bill of materials), listing all the elements that go to make a product or service; **a schedule of capacity**, showing the capacity the organization has to make things; and a list of current stock.

The essential MRP structure is shown in the next figure.

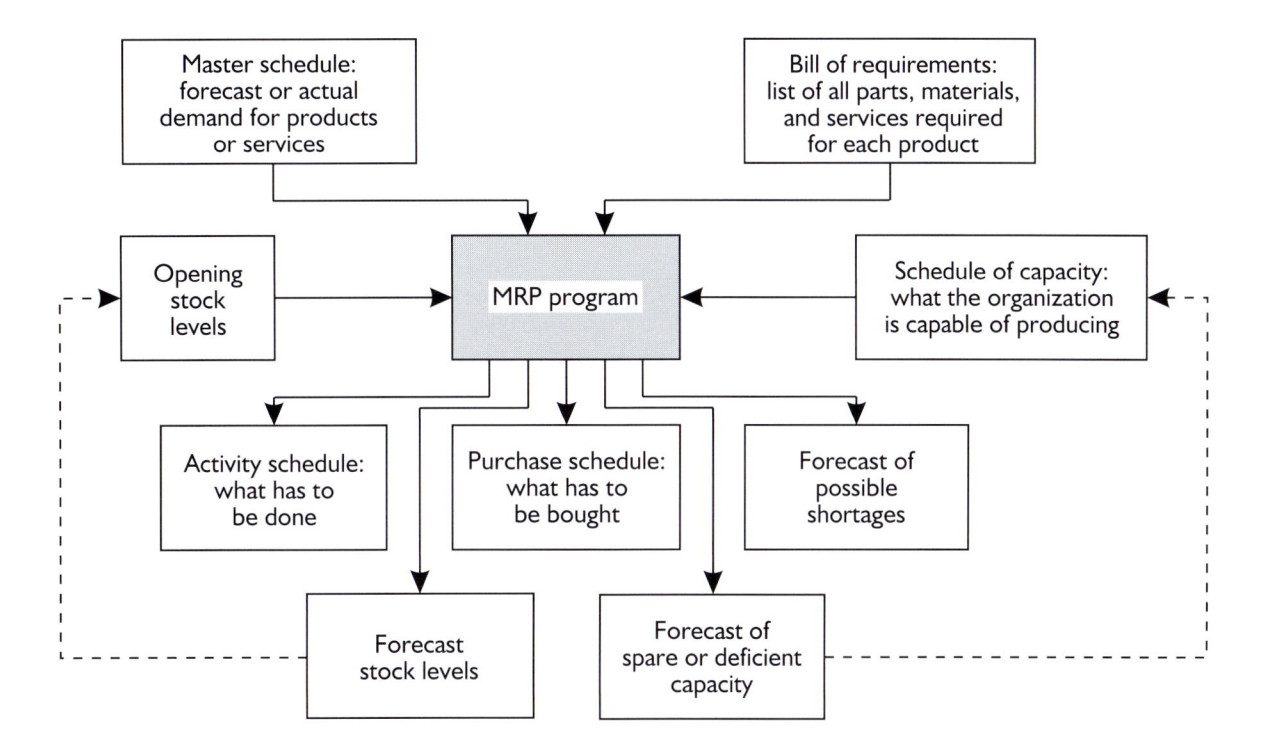

```
                Master schedule:                    Bill of requirements:
                forecast or actual                  list of all parts, materials,
                demand for products                 and services required
                   or services                        for each product
                         │                                   │
                         ▼                                   ▼
    Opening                                                        Schedule of capacity:
     stock    ─────────▶   MRP program   ◀─────────              what the organization
    levels                                                        is capable of producing
                         │         │        │
          ┌──────────────┤         │        └──────────────┐
          ▼              ▼         ▼                       ▼
   Activity schedule:   Purchase schedule:           Forecast of
     what has to         what has to                  possible
       be done           be bought                   shortages
                  │              │
                  ▼              ▼
              Forecast        Forecast of
            stock levels     spare or deficient
                              capacity
```

The centre box in this diagram is labelled the **MRP program** because the calculations are done by a software program on a computer. As with all computer programs, the accuracy of what you get out depends entirely on the accuracy of what you put in.

The program is run repeatedly, as new input data arrives.

Provided all the input data is correct, MRP is a very efficient method of scheduling and planning materials management. Prior to its use, materials and work scheduling was based on historical statistics, which was much less reliable.

**Session C**

# 4 Resource planning and management

Materials requirements planning was first introduced in the late 1980s at a time when only key areas of business were computerized – and 'computerized' meant specially written software running on mini or mainframe computers.

However, the introduction of low-cost networked PCs in the early 1990s opened up the possibility of linking up the activities of many more parts of the organization, and since that time we have seen steady advances in computerized methods of resource planning.

## 4.1 Manufacturing Resource Planning

As the name suggests, Manufacturing Resource Planning (sometimes called MRPII to distinguish it from MRP) does much more than simply plan materials requirements. Introduced in the early 1990s, it was a method for planning **all** manufacturing resources. Its starting point was the organization's business plans, and its outputs were detailed instructions for:

- the purchase department;
- suppliers;
- stores;
- the production staff.

In addition MRPII provided detailed financial plans, such as budgets and links to the financial accounting system.

MRPII software, together with networked PCs, linked together various, previously isolated functions, allowing manufacturing managers to obtain a complete picture of the activity and to set about optimising the way the activity was performed.

In non-manufacturing industries similar approaches were adopted to help manage core areas.

**Session C**

## 4.2 Enterprise Resource Planning

As the effectiveness of various parts of a business was transformed, the spotlight shifted to the overall efficiency of the entire enterprise. As the technology of PC networking developed, the possibilities of supporting a larger version of MRPII, covering the entire enterprise, became more obvious.

Enterprise Resource Planning (ERP) offered the opportunity to share common data, and therefore the resources contained within the data, across a wide range of common activities, promising to repeat on an enterprise-wide basis the improvements gained in individual areas of activity.

Typical components of an ERP system are as follows.

- Sales and distribution

  This covers order entry and delivery scheduling. This module also checks on product availability to ensure timely delivery, and checks the customer's credit status.

- Business planning

  This consists of demand forecasting; planning of product production and capacity; and detailed routing information that describes where and in what sequence the product is actually made.

- Production planning

  Once the Master Production Schedule is complete, that data is fed into the MRP (Materials Requirements Planning) module: we looked at these earlier.

- Shop floor control

  The planned orders from the MRP module are converted to production orders. This leads to production scheduling, dispatching, and job costing.

- Logistics

  This system takes care of the rest, assuring timely delivery to the customer. Logistics in this case consists of inventory and warehouse management, and delivery. The purchasing function is also usually grouped under logistics.

EXTENSION 5
Quayle and Jones' book looks at logistics from the point of view of those working in the distribution industry.

**Session C**

## Activity 31

*4 mins*

ERP systems have often failed to deliver the expected benefits when first implemented. Imagine that your organisation is planning to adopt ERP. What possible problems might arise?

_____

_____

_____

_____

People are often the biggest barrier to the success of a new system. Staff may take the view that what they were doing before worked perfectly well and either not use the new system, or insist that it is adapted to reflect their old way of doing things, in which case few of the benefits of integration will be realised. Office politics may have a part to play in this.

Individuals also have much more responsibility when systems are closely integrated. The consequences of a mistake in one department are no longer restricted to that department: the implications could be much more widespread.

Another major problem is that existing systems in individual departments may not be compatible with each other. Short of throwing away all the data in one of the systems or re-entering vast amounts of data there may be no easy way of making different systems 'talk' to each other, or at least not at acceptable cost. (Some software vendors have developed Enterprise Application Integration, or EAI, to address such problems.)

You may have thought of other ideas specific to your own organisation.

## 4.3 Supply Chain Management

Resource planning does not start and finish at the boundaries of the enterprise, so the next logical step has been to bring suppliers into the model at one end, and customers at the other end.

A 'supply chain' is a term used to describe how products or services move from an initial customer order through the various stages of obtaining any raw materials needed, putting them through production processes, and finally distributing the finished item to the customer. Numerous independent firms may be involved in a supply chain, for example manufacturers, components suppliers, delivery agents or shippers, wholesalers and retailers. Managing the chain of events in this process is called 'supply chain management'.

You may think that ERP software, as described above, covers the 'total material flow', but Supply Chain Management (SCM) software goes further. Although ERP systems provide a great deal of planning capabilities, the various material, capacity, and demand constraints are all considered separately, in relative isolation to each other.

SCM software helps to plan and optimize the supply chain as a continuous and seamless activity. SCM products are able to consider demand, capacity and material constraints simultaneously, and to perform real-time adjustments. Changes can be communicated instantaneously to all participants in the supply chain using Internet technology.

To give you a sense of the full capabilities of SCM software here is a list of the modules found in a typical SCM product from PeopleSoft.

| | | |
|---|---|---|
| Activity-Based Management | e-Procurement | Production Planning |
| Billing | e-Product Management | Promotions Management |
| Bills and Routings | e-Supplier Connection | Purchasing |
| Collaborative Supply Management | Flow Production | Quality |
| Cost Management | Inventory/Inventory Planning | SCM Portal Pack |
| Demand Planning | Order Management | Services Procurement |
| e-Bill Payment | Order Promising | Strategic Sourcing |
| Engineering | Product Configurator | Supply Chain Warehouse |
| Enterprise Planning | Production Management | Trading Partner Management |

The idea of Supply Chain Management is not new – it was first mooted by Michael Porter in the 1980s – but the ability to micro-manage it in large organizations has only become a reality thanks to relatively recent developments in information and communications technology.

**Session C**

Moreover, in a modern business, supply chain management is more than just a piece of software. It is a change of attitude.

In the past the supply chain was typically defined by antagonistic relationships.

- The purchasing function sought out the lowest-price suppliers, often through a process of tendering, the use of 'power' and the constant switching of supply sources to prevent getting too close to any individual source.
- Supplier contracts featured heavy penalty clauses and were drawn up in a spirit of general mistrust of all external providers.
- The knowledge and skills of the supplier could not be exploited effectively: information was deliberately withheld in case the supplier used it to gain power during price negotiations.

Hence, no single supplier ever knew enough about the ultimate customer to suggest ways of improving the cost-effectiveness of the trading relationship, for instance buying additional manufacturing capacity or investing in quality improvement activities.

It is now recognised that successful supply chain management is based upon collaboration and offers benefits to an organization's suppliers as well as to the organization itself. By working together, organisations can make a much better job of satisfying the requirements of their end market, and thus both can increase their market share.

- Organizations seek to enter into partnerships with key customers and suppliers so as to better understand how to provide value and customer service.
- Organizations' product design processes include discussions that involve both customers and suppliers. By opening up design departments and supply problems to selected suppliers a synergy results, generating new ideas, solutions, and new innovative products.
- To enhance the nature of collaboration the organization may reward suppliers with long term sole sourcing agreements in return for a greater level of support to the business and a commitment to on-going improvements of materials, deliveries and relationships.

**Session C**

## Activity 32

*4 mins*

One of the main motivations for introducing Supply Chain Management will be financial. What do you think might be typical financial impact for an organization of SCM in terms of revenue and costs?

_____

_____

_____

_____

Here are some ideas that you may have included in your answer.

- Reduced stock holding costs.
- Reduced costs of purchasing.
- Less waste because of better understanding of quality standards, and fewer errors.
- Increased revenue due to higher quality product.
- Increased revenue due to better/faster delivery performance.
- Increased revenue due to new product ideas and products that more closely match customer needs.

Now we move onto security.

# 5 Security

Security for home and family is a basic human aspiration. An attack on home or family, having property stolen and personal financial information rifled and misused are amongst people's worst nightmares. Similar fears haunt the managers of all organizations.

**Session C**

## 5.1 Types of security threats

If security fails it can affect employees, who may lose their jobs or even their lives as a result. So it is in *all* employees' interests to help employers create a secure working environment. The theft of physical property or physical harm to 'human resources' are evident from missing goods or injuries. Less obvious, but potentially more 'threatening' to the organization, is the theft of vital information, which is its very lifeblood.

## Activity 33 · 3 Minutes

Think of two examples of threats that can arise to the security of each of the following.

1 Physical property

2 People

3 Information or 'data'

When you think about it, you'll discover that there are many possibilities. You may have included some of the following possible threats.

- Theft by customers or employees; attack by other creatures, such as insects, birds, rodents; destruction or damage by fire or flooding.
- Assault by robbers, other staff, or the general public; injury caused by defective buildings or equipment; damage to wellbeing from hazardous substances, fumes, fire or flood. 'Poaching' of key employees by competing organizations.

## Session C

- Industrial espionage – theft of trade secrets; copying of materials; confidential records, e.g. costings; management accounts; personnel records; commercially sensitive information such as discounts allowed to major customers; proposed activities that might affect share prices; the despoiling of information deliberately by the introduction of computer viruses.

The possibilities are infinite and businesses are increasingly vulnerable for some or all of the following reasons.

- The size of manufacturing plants, distribution warehouses and stores increases. The loss of one 'key site' or plant can be ruinous if you've nowhere as large to fall back on.
- The decreasing 'tolerance threshold' of some people makes them a threat to employees in contact with the general public, such as in hospitals, transport/leisure facilities and shops.
- Information stored (and retrievable) electronically is highly portable and also prone to attack by computer hackers – think how much data can be stored on one floppy disk.

A major fire, the theft of a payroll, or the death of key personnel in a transport accident will have serious consequences. But it is statistically more probable that an organization will suffer the theft of information; or unauthorized use, malicious corruption or destruction of that information. Data held electronically is potentially accessible to **anyone, anywhere** in the world.

## Commercial secrets

Over the centuries, organisations have guarded zealously 'trade secrets' such as recipes, industrial processes and trading terms given to customers. For example, some recipes have been handed down through the generations and their knowledge restricted to the fewest possible employees

But, someone has to have the recipe for a product to be made – and if it is made by computer controlled equipment, the chances are that somewhere it will appear in an electronic memory which will not endure torture unto death to protect it!

**Session C**

## Activity 34

*3 mins*

Picture the following breaches of security and suggest the adverse consequences that might arise for the organization suffering them.

1 the weatherproofing of a third world country grain warehouse is breached by rodents

_____

_____

2 the sales manager of a commercial company is enticed to work for their major competitor

_____

_____

3 the payroll arrangements for distributing wages paid in cash to a multi-site retail company are accessed by a disgruntled former employee

_____

_____

Obviously, the consequences could be very serious in all three events.

> This workbook is not mainly concerned with the risks to health and safety, which are dealt with fully in 'Managing Lawfully – Health Safety & Environment'

- At its worst, there could be destruction of grain stocks by the rodents or by fire if they have damaged electrical wiring. That could lead to starvation for people already vulnerable through hunger. Whose responsibility would that be – the rodents or the people managing the grain store?
- The sales manager will have confidential information about trading terms, possibly company production methods and recipes, plus personal contacts and standing with major customers.
- Unauthorised access to payroll data may have helped the competitor make the sales manager an 'offer not to be refused'. This could lead to a major theft, or series of thefts if the employee chooses to share the information with criminals. If the criminals are armed, serious injury or death could result as well as loss of property.

These simple examples show that security lapses don't all come from deliberate theft and that one breach of security can easily lead to another – like a game of Consequences, which is really a light-hearted approach to risk management.

**Session C**

## 5.2 Risk management approaches to security

Professional risk management is the best defence against security lapses. It is also used in the health and safety arena, where you may already have encountered it. Below is a five-step approach.

### Five step approach to assessing and minimising risks to resources

1. **Identify** the resources at risk.

2. **Assess** the **probability** that the risk will be realized.

3. **Evaluate** the consequences.

4. **Prioritize** the consequences.

5. **Implement** a strategy to eliminate or minimize the risks – tackling the worst first

There is a major difference, however, between safety and security. Safety is concerned with hazard, while security deals with the intrinsic vulnerability of resources.

### Hazard

In safety management, hazard is the intrinsic potential of anything to cause harm, such as the capacity of asbestos fibres to cause fatal or serious illness.

In safety risk management, the recommended Health & Safety Executive approach says: *eliminate the hazard and you will eliminate the risk*, e.g. find a way of replacing asbestos with an entirely different material which achieves the same degree of thermal insulation but is not hazardous.

### Vulnerability

In security management, hazard becomes the **intrinsic vulnerability** of the resource, for example:

- the direct financial value of materials like diamonds, CDs, alcohol or cigarettes;
- the difficulty of replacing key buildings and equipment;

**Session C**

- the skills, knowledge and 'marketability' of people;
- the worth of data to a competitor or organization you may have to negotiate with.

Intrinsic vulnerability is necessary. You can eliminate hazard, but you can't eliminate intrinsic vulnerability without destroying the organisation's ability to function.

If your business is manufacturing industrial diamonds, or CDs, you cannot eliminate them from it. If you did replace the vulnerable resource, the replacement is likely to be as vulnerable as the item it replaces, but you **can** assess the risks to it and follow through the five-step process to eliminate or minimise the risks.

## 5.3 Using risk management to safeguard personnel; stock; equipment and data

You can apply the five-step approach in two ways: first to each resource individually and secondly for activities where the resources overlap.

You'll be asked to look at each in turn during this session.

### The invaluable 'what if' question

Implicit in all risk management is the simple but powerful question 'what if?' It is easy to remember and excellent for assessing the potential consequences of any risk, or series of risks, to all resources.

Look at it applied in several different situations

- 'What if' we open our restaurant after the local pub closes. Is there a risk to our staff from customers who have had too much to drink?
- 'What if' we go over to self service in our shops. Could it increase 'shrinkage' and negate the planned savings in staff wages?
- 'What if' we allow employees to take equipment home to work with. Is there a greater risk of it being damaged or stolen?
- 'What if' there is a fire at our payroll bureau. Do we, and/or they, have back up information available that is right up to date?

You can ask yourself the 'what if' question in any security management situation for two different reasons.

- As a short-cut way of assessing risks before implementing the full five-step analysis.

**Session C**

- As a way of reviewing a security strategy already implemented. It could be that a previously unconsidered potential risk has arisen, or changes to procedures are being considered.

Use the grid provided as Extension 6 to make an assessment of the security risks in the following scenario. Ask yourself the 'what if' question about all aspects of the scenario.

## Activity 35  *15 mins*

EXTENSION 6
Format for making five-step approach to security risk assessments

A cash and carry warehouse is just extending a branch and has asked you as the responsible manager to conduct a security risk assessment before the work starts. During the three month project, up to 20 contractors' staff will be working on site and will have to gain access via the main staff entrance and existing warehouse. Some overhead work will be involved and, at some stage, the contractors will need to break through the existing external wall, close to some high storage racking. The main computer terminal will have to be moved to a new office. It has been agreed that contractors staff can use company fork lift trucks, provided that they are licensed drivers and obtain formal permission from you on every occasion. Of the 50 company staff on site, around 40 are paid in cash on Thursday afternoons.

In the limited time available, make your assessment and indicate the strategy you would use to minimise each risk you identify

At the Glastonbury Festival in 2002, a high security fence was erected around a wide perimeter to prevent 'gatecrashers' entering the event without paying. As this is an open air event in a large space, there is less potential conflict with safety issues than in, for example, an upstairs dance hall.

You will find a model solution in the reflect and review session (on page 118).

There is no '100% right' solution in this situation, any more than there is in real life situations you may face at work. So, your solution may differ in some respects from the 'model'. The Activity will have given you some experience of the process of assessing risks and of deciding what the priorities should be for tackling the consequences identified.

## 5.4 The security versus safety conflict

Although there are similarities in approaches to security and safety, there are also potential conflicts. There can be a real struggle between the need to achieve maximum security and the priority to protect the lives of people who may be inadvertently 'imprisoned' by security measures. Some terrible losses

**Session C**

of life have occurred in stores, sports arenas, nightclubs and dance halls, where security devices prevented the victims escaping. It is understandable that owners of premises wish to control access and prevent gatecrashers getting in without paying (this is effectively a form of theft) but it is completely unacceptable, morally or legally, to risk people's lives in the attempt to achieve 100% security.

Often, problems are caused by security bars and locked or blocked emergency exits which prevent people escaping when a fire has started, or when a panic has caused people to stampede towards the exits. When people are shopping, working or sleeping upstairs, as in a department store, hospital or hotel, they are especially vulnerable.

## Minimizing the risks to personnel and visitors

There can be no greater risk to the security of personnel and visitors than finding themselves on the third floor, with the fire exits and windows securely barred in front of them as the spreading smoke and flames begin to overtake them.

Simple, but effective safeguards for all upstairs rooms demand that:

- there are at least two safe ways out, which are well separated and not dependant on lifts that cannot be used in emergencies;
- all emergency exits can be opened rapidly from the inside and are kept clear of obstructions on the outside.

## 5.5 Common sense security

> A labourer on a building site was challenged several times by a security guard as he passed through the gate pushing wheelbarrow loads. All the contents of the barrow proved to be worthless and bore out his claim that he was taking rubble to an off-site skip. It transpired that he had stolen ten wheelbarrows. This frequently told story does illustrate how simple strategies often defeat security systems.

The five-step risk management approach is a well proven, professional means of assuring security. However, it should not prevent you looking for simple, common sense ways to protect property against theft.

Look at the following case study, based on real events

### Example

A heavy goods vehicle driver, wearing an overall displaying a company logo, walked up to a fork lift driver in the despatch warehouse of a large company. He said he couldn't find anyone on the loading bay to load his vehicle and would they please help. At the bay, he indicated the largest of the assembled palletised loads – some ten tons of material, which they helped him to load. He thanked them politely for their help, secured his load and drove off, never to be seen again.

The driver arrived when most people, including the area's team leader, were on their lunch-break. He spoke politely and confidently to the staff and appeared to be in no hurry. There was a security gate, but it wasn't the only way out of the site. The load he took was worth several thousand pounds.

Very often, the simplest strategies are the most effective for a thief. Looking confident, appearing to know the way around and even asking for help can be much simpler, safer and more profitable than using dynamite, tunnels or guns. Such simple methods may even gain the thief grudging admiration for impudence and audacity.

But it affects the profitability of the business and, if repeated often enough, the security of employees' jobs can be jeopardised.

## Activity 36

*5 Mins*

Think about your own working area from a security perspective. Imagine that you are a potential thief on the lookout for easy pickings and think what you might be able to steal.

It will help you to use two of the concepts already introduced in this session.

> When you have decided on your priorities, be careful with whom you discuss them and where you put the list. Just in case any weaknesses you identify come to the knowledge of the 'wrong' people

1 *Vulnerability* – which items are most vulnerable to theft, through high value and portability? Remember to look at tools and raw materials that you use, as well as stocks of finished goods.

2 *What if* – ask yourself this question over matters such as changes of personnel; changes in working methods; storage facilities; suppliers; siting of entrances & exits; goods receipt and despatch systems – anything which could affect the security of materials, especially the most vulnerable to theft.

Draw up a list of priorities for discussion with your boss.

## Restricting access

Preventing people from entering areas where they do not need to be almost certainly figured in your list and in the arrangements for your own workplace.

It makes sense to classify areas into **low**, **medium**, **high** and **restricted categories**, with increasingly stringent access requirements including passes,

**Session C**

passwords and keys, swipe cards or security guards for the highest categories.

However, there are many organisations that find this approach difficult to implement fully. Hospitals, shops and shopping centres, leisure facilities, hotels, restaurants, airports, railway stations, amongst others, cannot bar the general public from many areas and indeed invite them to come in. For example, if you are going to see a relative in hospital, you will not wish to go through draconian security procedures taking 20 minutes to complete, yet the hospital will have large amounts of vulnerable materials including drugs on its site.

Even in the most secure sites where there is no public access, security systems in place have been designed by the 'wit of man' and so can be unravelled by the 'wit of man'. Locks, bars, photo cells and all the technical devices may achieve nothing if the local area supervisor doesn't challenge an official looking visitor who seems unfamiliar, or a security guard whose face is unknown.

## Careless talk

There was a famous World War Two poster which showed a scene in a pub, or some other place where people had the chance to chat to one another. Above the scene it said simply:

'CARELESS TALK COSTS LIVES.'

Large numbers of people – including yourself – need access to information that is confidential. It may be vital to you doing the job, but it could lead to breaches of security if seen or heard by the wrong people.

Here are some examples of information made freely available to outsiders, by employees who did not ask themselves: 'What is the security risk if this got into the wrong hands?

### Example

'We always take the money to the bank at 3 pm. If we don't, there's hell to pay from the retail manager.' (Shop manageress, talking to distribution driver whom she had kept waiting.)

'The payroll van comes along at 4 o'clock on a Wednesday afternoon, regular as clockwork'. (Wages office, talking to stranger complaining about access to site.)

'The safety officer insisted we removed the bars from that office window. He said we must find a safer way, though we've not found one yet' (heard in local pub, near to large store).

# Session C

> 'It's not been announced yet, but that site will be closing next month, so we're re-routing all the vehicles ready for when it happens.' (Distribution depot – talking about customer's site where more than 200 jobs would be lost).

## Security risks from written documents – paper and electronic

Computer screens often display confidential information about personnel, costings, payroll and financial matters to anyone who cares to read them. This happens in open plan offices and even in reception areas where the receptionist doubles as a clerical employee. Receptionists may also then have to discuss confidential matters over the internal phone system within earshot of visitors. The extensive use of faxes and emails increases the availability of information. An envelope marked 'confidential' or 'to be opened by addressee only' at least creates a physical barrier and anyone who reads it without authorisation knows they could be in trouble, whereas a fax coming through in a general office may be read by anyone, and an email circulated without need to a dozen people may end up giving information to dozens more, just like a chain letter.

Here are some real examples of security breaches from written documents.

### Example

An engineering company made an unauthorised video of reconditioned equipment installed on a manufacturing site. No-one on the shop floor challenged them, as they were so used to seeing engineers from the company around. The video included shots of a monitor screen displaying a secret recipe. (The engineers, to be fair, did not realise its significance.) They used the video for marketing purposes and the recipe was seen by a rival manufacturer who was also buying from the same engineers. It was secret no longer!

The personnel director of a company employing tens of thousands of people was horrified to find that a union official with whom he was negotiating knew his final offer position to the fraction of a penny. He surmised later that the national negotiator was adept at reading writing upside down and had read it from his notes. That cost his company dearly at the year's wages settlement. The following year, he relied on his memory!

**Session C**

> A major company was rumoured strongly to be planning a move from London to a town 20 miles away, certainly entailing many redundancies. The rumours were hotly denied. Then, a headline appeared in the financial press, giving full details of the move. The information was accurate. It transpired that an estate agent dealing with the acquisition was married to someone who worked in public relations for the company that was moving and had warned the spouse – who had let it slip to a contact on the newspaper which then published the story.

None of these real life examples involved any complicated technology or code cracking ability. Preventing them required only the use of basic common sense security approaches and personal integrity – costing nothing. But they cost the organisations involved dearly in terms of both cash and embarrassment.

## The 'need to know' principle

This commonly applied security principle says simply that information should be provided to people on the basis that they 'need to know' it in order to do their job. In hierarchical terms, the 'higher' you climb up the management ladder, the more information you probably need to know.

Directors normally have access to all or most information, but even here, data such as discount levels to major customers, may be restricted.

Does the production director 'need to know' what override discounts are given, or the sales director the tentative 'final offer' decided on for this year's wages review? Probably not, and the fewer people who know, the less chance is there that they will tell anyone else, deliberately or accidentally.

In reality, many people at *all* levels in the hierarchy 'need to know' a great deal of confidential information and, ultimately, have to behave in a trustworthy fashion. This creates potential problems in open plan areas, including those in offices, banks, building societies and shops.

**Session C**

## Activity 37

*5 mins*

Underline the confidential information which each occupation in the following list probably 'needs to know' to do the job. Be strict in your interpretation.

1 Wages and salaries clerk:
 cash payroll delivery arrangements; basic salary and commission rates for sales staff; details of forthcoming pay offer.

2 Sales representative:
 annual override discounts for major customers; details of most profitable lines to sell; credit ratings for each customer.

3 Mixing machine operator:
 recipes for specialist products; costs of all ingredients used; total costs of producing lines for which mixes are provided.

4 Checkout sales assistant:
 details of promotional offers; gross margins on all lines sold; arrangements for banking cash at local branch.

5 Team leader for the distribution planning department:
 wages costs for delivery driver; profit margins on each product distributed; fuel costs of using different types of vehicle.

You will probably have come very close to the model answer, though you might disagree on some points.

1 A wages and salaries clerk probably needs to know only basic salary and commission rates for sales staff.

2 A sales representative probably needs to know details of 'most profitable' lines to sell and credit ratings for each customer.

3 A mixing machine operator probably needs to know recipes for specialist products and costs of all ingredients used.

4 A checkout sales assistant probably needs to know only details of promotional offers.

5 A team leader for the distribution planning department probably needs to know only the fuel costs of using different types of vehicle.

87

**Session C**

### The need for integrity

Most people enjoy the feeling that they know something which others don't – 'knowledge is power' is an oft repeated truism. It is also true that many people enjoy 'letting slip' some of the knowledge which they have, for whatever reason. This is where many breaches of security arise.

■ In the example of the company moving its office, the breach occurred when one spouse warned the other that their job might be at risk. This happened even though the information imparted was supposed to be completely confidential to the estate agency and senior staff in the company for whom they were acting.

It is easy to let slip information in social situations and it is often difficult to know where the communications line will end. It can move like a geometric progression where:

1  A tells B something – so now two people know
2  B tells C and D – so now four people know
3  C and D each tell two other people (E, F and G, H) – so now eight people know.
4  E, F, G and H each tell two other people – so now 16 people know.

The 'confidential' information will soon spread to dozens more. Whether or not that matters depends on what those people do with it, apart from telling other people.

But, the more people who know something sensitive, such as confidential plans for major changes to an organization, the more likely it becomes that it will be used in a way which harms the organization and the interests of both it and its employees.

Your team will look to you for an example in this area of management and will respect you more if you don't breach the confidence you have been trusted with.

## 5.6 Insurance

It is often believed that damage to property, or theft of stock, or damage to equipment, doesn't matter that much because 'the insurer will pay up'. This is wrong, for a number of reasons.

### The iceberg principle

Just like an iceberg, many aspects of a loss insured against are below the surface. While the direct costs of replacing a wrecked asset or stolen goods may be covered, many others below the surface are not, typically:

**Session C**

- loss of productive time;
- loss of morale – especially where injuries have occurred;
- diversion of management time;
- the cost of hiring or training replacement staff;
- loss of business, either short term or long term;
- legal costs.

Even for the items covered by insurance, over time, premiums will increase to reflect the claims record of the organisation, just as happens to a private car driver with a poor accident record.

The more far-sighted organizations now look at losses due to breaches of security just like any other business cost, and include them amongst the factors by which they judge managers' performance levels. Some will not insure some aspects of their activities where there is no legal requirement to do so. Instead, they require managers to control the costs of security just like raw material costs, fuel costs or commission to sales staff.

## The moral and legal dimensions

Insurance does not deal with the moral obligations to protect staff, customers and visitors from harm, increasingly backed by the threat of legal action which can lead to substantial fines or even imprisonment. Those which will **not** be insurable risks.

## Company property

Some employees believe that theft of company or organization's property – or damage to it – doesn't matter as the costs are borne by the management or some impersonal organization which has infinite amounts of money.

But no organization is prepared to keep replacing assets that are stolen or wrecked by misuse. There is always another option, which could involve buying in materials from elsewhere, or ultimately the closure of a site that is proving too costly to run. This has happened to retail stores where more stock was apparently leaving via the staff exit than through the checkouts.

It is also over optimistic, to say the least, to believe that dishonest people will distinguish between the cash and property of individuals and that of the organisation. It may be taboo to 'shop' people known to be pilfering goods or money from the organization, but, there is a real risk that staff who will not help catch them will find themselves the victim of crime, or reckless behaviour.

The mistaken belief that theft or abuse of the organization's property is not important is one that you should address regularly when talking to your team members. Remind them that there are direct and indirect risks to their personal prosperity and that it is not in any of their interests for the organisation to fail.

**Session C**

## 5.7 Malicious attack

It is a regrettable fact that violence at work has increased in recent years. The figures vary from one workplace to another, with some much more prone than others.

### Activity 38 · 3 mins

> Around 20% of UK employees have been physically threatened whilst at work. In other countries, the figures are much worse. In the USA, the most frequent cause of death for female employees is murder.

This list includes five of the workplaces that have the worst records for violence at work. Which do you think they are? Underline five.

1 Petrol retailers

2 Hotels and guest houses

3 DHSS benefits offices

4 Pubs

5 Nightclubs

6 Shopping centres

7 Hospitals

8 Sports centres

9 Restaurants

The answers to this activity may or may not surprise you, depending on where you work and spend your leisure time. The following five workplaces have the worst record for violence at work:

- petrol retailers;
- DHSS benefits offices;
- pubs;
- nightclubs;
- hospitals.

**Session C**

The one ambiguous category is probably shopping centres. As a whole, they are not the riskiest places, but many individual outlets are right at the top of the list, whether in shopping centres or on high streets, especially those selling:

- alcohol;
- jewellery;
- electrical goods, which are of high value, portable and have a ready market through illegal outlets of various kinds.

### Who are the attackers?

Customers or users of services in places, such as hospital accident and emergency wards, are by far the most frequent offenders. Outsiders generally are the next most frequent assailants, with work colleagues the least likely attackers.

> Analyses of assaults on employees at work show that around 40% of assaults are by customers, 25% by outsiders, including criminals, and 20% by colleagues

## 5.8 Using the five-step approach to risk assessment in practice

Now that we have looked in detail at a variety of security risks, we will look at the five-step approach to risk assessment more closely, by applying it to the problem of malicious attack.

How prone your organisation is to attack will depend on what you do and where you do it. You need to do a proper risk assessment following the five-step approach.

1   **Identify** the resources at risk. In this case, you know that the resource at risk is the human one.

2   **Assess** the **probability** that the risk will be realized. This will depend on the circumstances, e.g. employees most probably at risk are those who:

- work alone and/or at nights, perhaps making security checks;
- work on remote sites;
- transport valuable merchandise;
- handle or transport cash at any stage;
- visit customers at home for any reason – especially if alone;
- deal with members of the general public who may be influenced by alcohol.

3   **Evaluate** the consequences. These could include serious injury or death

**Session C**

4   **Prioritise** the consequences. You will need to look at which employee, or category of employees, is most at risk. Take account of all the evidence that exists for the field you work in, from similar organisations, trade bodies and government sources.

5   **Implement** a strategy to eliminate or minimise the risks, tackling the worst first. Remember that all individuals or groups at risk of serious injury must be given equal top priority.

## Implementing a strategy for risk reduction

Now, follow through the fifth step in detail: Implement a strategy to eliminate or minimise the risk, with **elimination** being the real aim where people are at risk.

As an example, look at the situation where an employee visits customers at home. Many employees do, including estate agents, meter readers, sales personnel, service engineers, social services personnel and nurses.

## A check list approach

A simple check list will help you to clarify the issues.

1   Is there another way of doing the job? If YES then IMPLEMENT IT and so eliminate the risk. If NO then continue through checklist.

2   Should some areas be declared 'out of bounds' for home visits? This decision can be based on previous experience and records.

3   Should some categories of people be refused home visits? This can be based on records/profiles of likely offenders.

4   Should we provide a second person as back up?

5   Have we provided suitable training for staff? Such training should include how to recognise and deal with signs of potential violence.

6   Do we have systems and equipment for checking where staff are and that they are safe at pre-determined intervals? Are they enforced at all times, including outside office hours.

7   Is suitable protective equipment required and is it available? Are staff trained to use it?

8   Have we sufficient expertise to create a secure system for ourselves? Should we consult outside experts?

**Session C**

Security issues are frequently complex and involve sensitive matters, especially where there could be a danger of injury to employees or even loss of life. Using the five-step approach followed by the checklist to develop your strategy will help you to ensure that important issues are not forgotten.

In this case, we considered the risk to people, but the same approach works for equipment, stock and data.

## 5.9 The costs of security

Security measures can be extremely expensive to implement. Eventually, the **cost** of achieving security may **equal or outweigh** the **value** of the resources being protected.

As this point approaches, organizations must ask themselves if each succeeding increase in cost is justifiable, or whether perhaps the activity is not viable and affordable.

Where people's lives are at risk, the issues become very complex and in general terms it is not legally or morally acceptable to say 'we'd like to improve their security, but we can't afford to'. In such circumstances, the eventual decision may be to eliminate the activity associated with the risk altogether, for example:

> Eurotunnel spent millions of pounds trying to protect its' Calais terminal from ingress by inmates of the nearby Sangatte refugee camp. On many occasions, trains were halted, or the whole operation paralysed for substantial periods. This security issue threatened the viability of an entire international transport operation with Europe-wide implications for rail and road traffic.

- by closing a restaurant **before** a local pub turns out customers who have a record of violent and offensive behaviour;
- by eliminating payment of wages in cash and persuading all employees to accept payment by bank transfer;
- by ceasing to stock lines that are constantly being stolen, or moving them to counter service rather than self service situations.

Security issues are seldom simple to manage. Elimination is not an option for the accident and emergency facility in an inner city hospital, at least not in this country, with its long and proud tradition of caring for the sick or injured, so, the only option is to **minimise the risks** and ensure that the people who face them are trained and equipped to face it.

## 5.10 Security policy

EXTENSION 7
This is a model security policy for you to compare with existing security policies.

While the most important factor in achieving security is the attitude and behaviour of employees at every level, it is good practice for all organizations to have a formal security policy.

93

**Session C**

## Activity 39

*15 mins*

**S/NVQ B1.2**

Look through the model security policy in extension 6.

1. If your organization already has a policy, compare it with the model. Are there differences? If there are, should your organization consider making any changes? Provide a one page summary of the differences you notice.

2. If your organization does not have a policy, consider if you should recommend introducing one to appropriate managers within your organization. Produce a draft based on the model.

## Self-assessment 3

*15 mins*

1. Fill in the missing words in the diagram below.

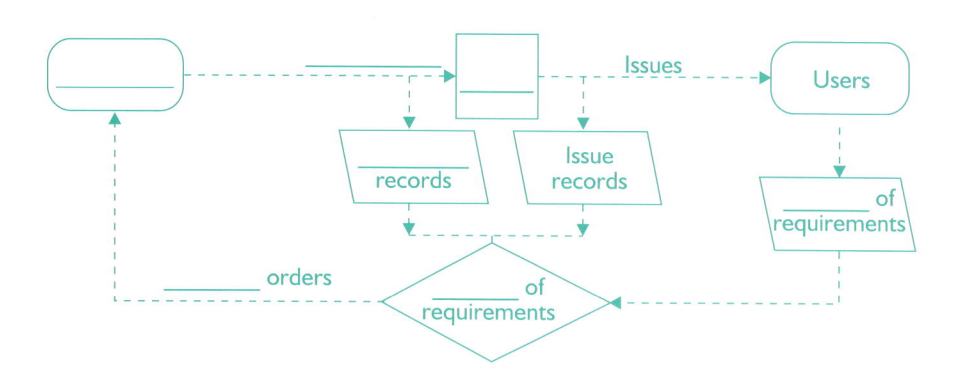

[Diagram: A flowchart with boxes showing a process. An unlabeled box connects to another unlabeled box, which "Issues" to "Users". There are "_____ records" and "Issue records" boxes. "Users" connects to "_____ of requirements". There is a "_____ of requirements" diamond and "_____ orders" flow.]

94

**Session C**

2 Match each name on the left with the correct comments, selected from the list on the right. More than one comment is associated with each name.

   A   Materials requirements planning (MRP)

   B   Electronic data interchange (EDI)

   C   Just-in-time (JIT)

   D   Automated guided vehicle (AGV)

   a   Enables buyers and suppliers to exchange a range of business documents including orders.
   b   Is concerned with the scheduling of activities and the management of stock.
   c   Is sometimes known as 'paperless trading'.
   d   May follow the path of wires laid beneath the floor.
   e   Produces schedules for activities and purchases as outputs.
   f   Produces forecast stock level as an output.
   g   Requires suppliers to make frequent deliveries, with very short lead-times.
   h   Enables the customer to minimize stocks held in a waiting area.
   i   Causes the customer's stock-holding costs to be passed to the supplier.
   j   Is typically employed in moving heavy or palleted goods.

3   a   What do you understand by the concept of vulnerability and how does it differ from hazard in risk assessments for safety?

    b   For many organisations, the worst security nightmare nowadays is the _____ or malicious _____ of _____ _____.

    c   Professional _____ _____ approaches are the best means of assuring the security of _____ _____ _____ and _____.

    d   Why is it important for an organisation to have a written security policy, made known to all employees ?

    e   Using the 'what if' question is a simple but effective way of _____ _____ of a risk minimisiation strategy.

    f   Customers and users of services account for _____ per cent of malicious attacks on _____.

95

**Session C**

# 6 Summary

- The functions of purchasing include:
    - finding new suppliers;
    - minimizing the cost of purchases;
    - arranging for goods to be delivered when and where they are needed;
    - maintaining good relations with suppliers and with other parts of the organization.

- Electronic Data Interchange (EDI) is now used by many companies to speed up and control the exchange of business documents required when goods are bought and sold. Originally requiring specialist hardware and software, it was very expensive to run, but EDI is now available much more cheaply using the resources of the Internet.

- E-procurement, or B2B, is now also widely used for the purchase of non-production goods such as office supplies.

- Some businesses are using the potential of technology to create alliances for purchasing common requirements.

- The just-in-time system aims to minimize stock holding, and to demand supplies at the time and place they are needed, but not before they are needed. The system is only a practical proposition for large organizations with considerable 'buying power'.

- MRP (materials requirements planning) is:
    - mainly concerned with the scheduling of activities, and the management of stock;
    - is most useful where components and sub-assemblies are produced, for inclusion in the final product or service.

- Inputs to an MRP program are: the master schedule; a bill of requirements; the opening stock balances; a schedule of capacity. Outputs are: an activity schedule; a purchase schedule; a shortage list; forecast stock levels; forecast of spare or deficient capacity.

- MRPII (manufacturing resources planning mark II) goes much further than MRP, in that it is a method for planning all manufacturing resources.

- Enterprise Resource Planning (ERP) looks at the potential for increasing efficiency by sharing common data across the whole enterprise.

- Supply Chain Management uses software to bring suppliers into the chain of management of materials and resources, thus optimizing the supply chain.

- Security management should flow from a clear statement of policy, backed with appropriate resources and proper organisation and arrangements, including training at all levels and the clear indication that disciplinary action will be taken against any employee who breaches the policy.

- Risk assessments and frequent use of the 'what if' question are essential elements of professional security management. The potential consequences of identified risks must be dealt with on the basis of tackling the 'worst first'

- Professional risk management will deter most potential offenders and save time in any investigations.

- The most important single aspect of security is the attitude of managers, who must set the right example to employees, contractors and customers at all times.

- Restricting access to stock and sensitive areas and disseminating information on the 'need to know' principle are important aspects of a security policy.

- Careless talk in an organizational security context can cost livelihoods.

- Complete security is an unachievable goal for any organization – the cost would outweigh the value of the savings achieved.

# Performance checks

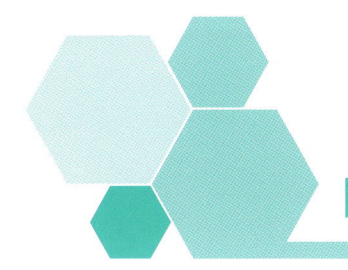

## 1 Quick quiz

Jot down the answers to the following questions on *Controlling Physical Resources*.

Question 1   We listed nine types of resource. Name **five** of these.

Question 2   Why might it be dangerous to treat people as just another resource?

Question 3   What would you say to someone who wanted some good general advice on getting the best from equipment?

**Performance checks**

Question 4    Explain the differences between raw materials, components and consumables.

Question 5    Explain briefly what is meant by the statement: 'having stocks too high is bad news; having stocks too low may be worse news'.

Question 6    What is meant by 'shrinkage'?

Question 7    Write down the book stock formula.

Question 8    What is the purpose of ABC analysis?

Question 9    Which **two** main types of transaction take place as a result of goods being received?

Question 10   What is the meaning of 'minimum stock'?

## Performance checks

**Question 11** 'There are no real advantages for an organization in having a person or group that specializes in purchasing.' Briefly explain the reasons why you do, or do not, agree with this statement.

_____
_____
_____

**Question 12** Name **one** advantage, and **one** disadvantage, of the just-in-time system, from the point of view of the organization being supplied.

_____
_____
_____

**Question 13** List **one** input, and **two** outputs, of an MRP program.

_____
_____
_____
_____

**Question 14** What do you understand by the 'need to know' principle?

_____
_____
_____

**Question 15** It is not legally or morally acceptable to reject expensive security measures when the _____ and _____ of people are involved.

**Question 16** What are the limitations of a 'restricted access' policy?

_____
_____
_____

Answers to these questions can be found on pages 119–20.

**Performance checks**

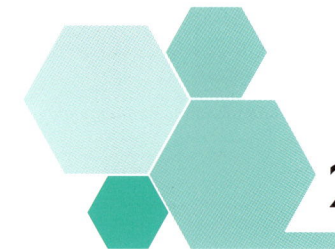

# 2 Workbook assessment

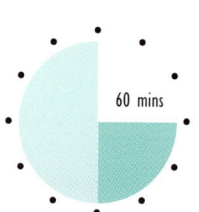

⏱ 60 mins

Read the following case incident and then deal with the questions that follow, writing your answers on a separate sheet of paper.

AC Electrics is an independent company that, in its one plant, produces about 150 different consumer products. In many cases, the difference between the products is only slight and the result of some modification. For example, they produce twelve models of vacuum cleaner.

The consumer market is extremely competitive and so it is essential, if it is to survive, for the firm to adopt a market-oriented policy. This is even more important for AC Electrics as they are one of the smaller firms in this business. To this end AC Electrics sell directly to wholesalers and large retailers throughout the country. These customers expect a high level of service and often require very fast deliveries. In order to meet these demands, AC Electrics established a number of regional warehouses, where stocks of all the products are held.

Three departments have responsibility for the control of stock.

- The marketing department is responsible for the control of all finished goods both in the warehouses and at the plant. Through their direct contacts with existing and prospective customers and their market-research activities, they claim to be able to forecast the stock levels required for each product in each warehouse.
- The production department is responsible for the control of stock required for production and also for work-in-progress. Production requirements consist mainly of bought-in components, together with a few raw materials such as packaging. The department's principal concern is to meet promptly the requirements of the marketing department to supply the regional warehouses. In order to meet this aim, production plans often have to be changed at relatively short notice.
- The other department which has responsibility for stocks within AC Electrics is the purchasing department; this is concerned with maintenance stocks and works and office supplies. It does the buying for the production department. The purchasing department

## Performance checks

> is not entirely happy with the short-term planning of the production department and its effect on purchasing costs. Generally, they believe that the organization is paying too much for components and materials, and that costs could be reduced if they could place orders in larger quantities.

1 Identify the likely costs associated with the above method of holding stocks.

2 Suggest **two** ways in which some of these costs might be reduced.

3 What advantages would AC Electrics gain by adopting a system of materials management such as MRP?

4 Do you think that stock-holding costs could be wholly or partly passed along to AC Electrics' suppliers? Explain your answer.

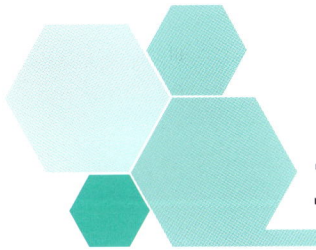

# 3 Work-based assignment

60 mins

S/NVQ B1.2

The time guide for this assignment gives you an approximate idea of how long it is likely to take you to write up your findings. You will find you need to spend some additional time gathering information, perhaps talking to colleagues and thinking about the assignment.

Your written response to this assignment should form useful evidence for your S/NVQ portfolio. The assignment is designed to help you to demonstrate your personal competence in:

- communicating;
- focusing on results;
- thinking and taking decisions.

**What you have to do**

Your aim is to put forward a concrete proposal designed to reduce your organization's costs related to the management of materials.

You may choose any aspect of the subject that we have discussed in this workbook. Then you will probably need to spend some time investigating and

101

## Performance checks

analysing the way things are done at present, and then identify an area where savings might be made. For example, you could examine the costs of shrinkage in the stores, or perhaps suggest that purchasing is carried out by a specialist, rather than by individual managers. Alternatively, you might look at documentation procedures.

If you aren't sure where to start, you might like to discuss possibilities with your tutor or your manager. If you want to look at an area outside your own sphere of control, no doubt you will have to seek permission from the relevant person first.

Write your work in the form of a short report, addressed to your manager, giving any evidence from the workplace that you have collected to support your findings.

# Reflect and review

## 1 Reflect and review

Now that you have completed your work on *Controlling Physical Resources*, let us review our workbook objectives.

This was our first objective.

- When you have completed this workbook you will be better able to contribute to the management and control of resources in your organization.

We have looked, if only briefly in some cases, at a number of resources, and have highlighted a number of associated problems. As a manager, one of your principal functions is to organize and control resources effectively and efficiently.

Although we didn't devote much space to the management of people in this workbook, a couple of very important points were noted: the difficulties of developing people to their full potential; and the dangers of regarding employees as inanimate objects, to be handled without respect for their dignity as human beings.

Equipment, land, buildings, and materials, all require careful management, and, in the case of the first three, we identified a few ways in which they might be usefully dealt with.

Our main concern, however, has been with materials, and we have considered many aspects of the management of this resource.

# Reflect and Review

You might like to think about the answers to the following questions.

- How could you increase your skills in the management of people?

- How could you set about finding out more about the management of some of the other resources mentioned: equipment, time, energy, finance, land, buildings, information?

- What will be your first step in contributing further to the control of resources in your organization?

The second objective was as follows.

- When you have completed this workbook you will be better able to explain the principles, and some ways of solving the problems, of stores and stock control.

The purpose of a store is as a buffer between the supplier and the user: between supply and demand. Holding stock, as we discussed, does not come cheap. In any small or medium-sized organization, however, it is an almost inescapable function. For large corporations, the costs and problems may be pushed onto the suppliers, using JIT.

Technology may help, and the increasing use of computers and other electronic devices, certainly enables organizations to reduce shrinkage and over-stocking. Useful techniques include those of ABC analysis, better documentation, and stock rotation. Everyday efficiency by teams and team leaders can do wonders for cost control.

# Reflect and Review

- Which of the stock control techniques described in the workbook might be appropriate for your organization? How might you investigate it further?

  _____
  _____
  _____

- Write down **one** problem in stores or stock control that you know about. How could you set about solving it?

  _____
  _____
  _____

The third objective was as follows.

- When you have completed this workbook you will be better able to increase your skills in various aspects of materials management.

Materials management entails much more than stores and stock control, and effective organizations take a broad-based view of the subject. Purchasing is one area: how can materials be obtained at minimum cost? In the production of goods and services, how can plans be made so that all operations run more efficiently? Would increased automation be an answer?

You may not be in a position to make large-scale plans for your organization, but you can try to improve the way things are run in your own work area, and you can take steps to increase your own knowledge and skills.

- What specific aspects of materials management should you study further? How will you go about doing this?

  _____
  _____
  _____

The final objective was as follows.

- When you have completed this workbook you will be better able to identify risks to physical, human and information resources and have gained some practical ideas and experience with which to guard against them.

All managers have a responsibility for the security of the resources which they manage, including the 'human' resources. You have had opportunity to look at a number of aspects of this vast subject, which perplexes not only commercial organisations but governments throughout the world, including the following.

105

## Reflect and Review

- The varied nature of security risks and their repercussions.
- The five-step risk management approach to security management and the use of 'what if' questions to help you plan for contingencies.
- The need to balance security considerations against the safety rights of people who need to escape rapidly from buildings.
- The need to apply 'common sense' strategies to prevent opportunist or audacious attempts to breach security.
- The restriction of access to premises, stocks and information to protect security.
- The mistake in believing that insurance means that losses 'don't matter' or that losses don't matter because 'it's only company property'.
- The increasing need to guard against malicious attacks on personnel.
- The costs v. savings balance and the threat of business closure when costs of security become unsustainable.
- The need for a security policy published to and applicable to personnel at all levels, backed up by the example which managers set to their staff at all times.

What specific messages will you take from this session and apply to make your own work area secure, or recommend for use more widely within your organisation?

_____

_____

_____

## 2 Action plan

Use this plan to further develop for yourself a course of action you want to take. Make a note in the left-hand column of the issues or problems you want to tackle, and then decide what you intend to do, and make a note in column 2.

The resources you need might include time, materials, information or money. You may need to negotiate for some of them, but they could be something easily acquired, like half an hour of somebody's time, or a chapter of a book. Put whatever you need in column 3. No plan means anything without a timescale, so put a realistic target completion date in column 4.

Finally, describe the outcome you want to achieve as a result of this plan, whether it is for your own benefit or advancement, or a more efficient way of doing things.

**Reflect and Review**

| Desired outcomes | | | | |
|---|---|---|---|---|
| | 1 Issues | 2 Action | 3 Resources | 4 Target completion |
| | | | | |
| Actual outcomes | | | | |

107

# Reflect and Review

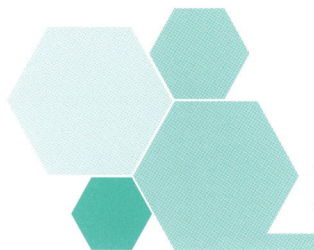

# 3 Extensions

**Extension 1**

| | |
|---|---|
| Book | *Storage and Supply of Materials* |
| Author | David Jessop and Alex Morrison |
| Edition | 6th edition, 1994 (7th edition due 2003) |
| Publisher | FT Prentice Hall |

Jointly published with the Chartered Institute of Purchasing and Supply, this book 'seems to be firmly established as the standard book for practitioners and students ... The contents have generally been brought up to date, with greater emphasis on health and safety and to relevant EC directives ...' It is not difficult to read, and would be very useful to have on hand as a reference book, and something to dip into when you have time.

**Extension 2**

| | |
|---|---|
| Standard | *BS EN ISO 9001:2000 Quality management systems. Requirements* |
| Publisher | British Standards Institution |

There was formerly a British Standard directly concerned with stock control (BS 5729) but this has been withdrawn, no doubt because it was published in the 1980s and bore little relation to current practice.

However, the latest version of the well-known international quality management standard, BS EN ISO 9001, contains a number of very relevant sections. There is more on this in the Super Series title *Achieving Quality*, but here is a brief note of the parts of BS EN ISO 9001 that are particularly relevant to controlling physical resources.

- **6.3 Infrastructure**
  This section contains requirements about maintaining buildings, workspaces, and equipment.
- **7.4.1 Purchasing process**
  This encourages organizations to set up controls to ensure that purchased products meet materials specifications and that their suppliers meet supplier selection criteria.
- **7.4.2 Purchasing information**
  These requirements encourage proper record-keeping. Purchasing documents should clearly describe the product ordered.
- **7.4.3 Verification of purchased product**
  This section sets out requirements to verify incoming materials at your own organization's premises and/or at the suppliers' premises. (Verify means to

perform whatever checks and tests are necessary to make sure that the purchased items meet your organisation's specifications.)

- **7.5.3 Identification and traceability**
  Purchases should be identifiable from the time they are received throughout all the stages of production, delivery and installation.
- **7.5.4 Customer property**
  This section reminds organizations to identify, verify and safeguard property supplied by their customers, for instance if the customer sends in a product for repair.
- **7.5.5 Preservation of product**
  This section requires you to take steps to avoid damage to products and components during production and on final delivery, for instance by using proper packaging, by refrigerating perishable items, or by handling fragile items with care.

**Extension 3**

Book　　　*Just in Time*
Author　　David Hutchins
Edition　　2nd Edition, 1999
Publisher　Gower Publishing Limited

Just In Time is not just another way of organising stock control, but a radical change in the production methods and in the role of employees. They have to take far more responsibility for production, which in turn requires their commitment and enthusiasm. This book looks at all these aspects and shows how the purchasing and stock control functions have to change to support JIT.

**Extension 4**

Book　　　*Essentials of Operations Management*
Author　　Ray Wild
Edition　　5$^{th}$ Edition, 2001
Publisher　The Continuum International Publishing Group

This book covers all aspects of the operations and production management function, with a number of useful case studies to show how it inter-relates to the purchasing, supply, logistics and materials handling functions, in the use of systems such as JIT, MRP and automated handling.

**Extension 5**

Book　　　*Logistics: an Integrated Approach*
Author　　Michael Quayle & Bryan Jones
Edition　　1998
Publisher　Liverpool Academic Press

Focusing on the supply chain from the physical distribution perspective, this book will be particularly useful to those people working in the distribution industry who want to develop their understanding of how their role relates to other supply chain functions.

**Reflect and Review**

Extension 6

| FIVE-STEP APPROACH TO ASSESSING AND MINIMISING SECURITY RISKS |||||
|---|---|---|---|---|
| **Brief description of situation** |||||
| | **RESOURCES AFFECTED** ||||
| | HUMAN | STOCK | EQUIPMENT | DATA |
| 1 Identify resources at risk | | | | |
| 2 Probability that risk will be realized | | | | |
| 3 Evaluate consequences | | | | |
| 4 Prioritize consequences | | | | |
| 5 Recommended strategy to eliminate or minimize the risks (tackling the 'worst first') | | | | |

**Extension 7**  **MODEL SECURITY POLICY**

### POLICY STATEMENT

It is the Policy of the _____ organisation to assure the security of its' human, physical and information resources against harm or abuse, however arising.

This Policy will apply to _____ property and that of all employees whilst on company premises, provided that they have complied with the security procedures for their areas.

### RESOURCES

The Chief Executive is responsible for ensuring that a level of resources is provided to eliminate or minimise each risk assessed commensurate with the consequences of the risks identified.

### RESPONSIBILITIES

**Board Level**
Overall responsibility for implementing this Policy rests with the _____ Executive.

**Management Level**
All Managers are required to take responsibility for their defined areas of operation.

**All employees**
Are required to act at all times with respect towards the property of the organisation, colleagues and all other people with whom they have dealings.

They must obey all reasonable instructions regarding security, including those concerning searches of vehicles, lockers and the person in accordance with the procedures agreed with staff representatives.

Employees and Managers at any level who flout security procedures, deliberately or recklessly, will be subject to disciplinary procedures which may lead to dismissal.

### RISK ASSESSMENT

This organisation will require all Managers to conduct formal Risk Assessments for their areas of responsibility, using the standard Organisation system in its' current edition.

Managers will be required to assign priorities to the risks identified for their areas.

- To deal directly with those for which they have adequate resources available.

# Reflect and Review

- To make recommendations and requests for assistance for resources for identified risks which they cannot deal with directly.

### TRAINING & SUPERVISION

The Organisation will provide appropriate training and supervision identified as necessary by the risk assessments provided:

- including training in the implementation of all matters relating to the implementation of this Policy.

### PUBLISHING AND UPDATING

The _____ Executive will be responsible for:

- publishing this policy throughout the organisation;
- updating it whenever necessary to keep it in accord with any legislation affecting it and with 'best practices' for this aspect of management.

**SIGNED** _____ **Chief Executive**

**DATED** _____ 2 _____ **EDITION No.** _____

These extensions can be taken up via your ILM Centre. They will either have them or will arrange that you have access to them. However, it may be more convenient to check out the materials with your personnel or training people at work – they may well give you access. There are other good reasons for approaching your own people; for example, they will become aware of your interest and you can involve them in your development.

# 4 Answers to self-assessment questions

**Self-assessment 1 on pages 19–20**

1 Compare your ticks with the table below.

|  | Materials | Equipment | People | Buildings | Land | Information | Energy | Finance | Time |
|---|---|---|---|---|---|---|---|---|---|
| Land |  |  |  |  | ✓ |  | ✓ |  |  |
| Capital | ✓ | ✓ |  | ✓ |  | ✓ |  | ✓ |  |
| Labour |  |  | ✓ |  |  |  |  |  | ✓ |

2 The complete list is as follows.

The management of resources involves:

1 **DECIDING** what you want to achieve;
2 making **PLANS** to achieve it;
3 **SPECIFYING** the necessary resources;
4 locating and **ACQUIRING** those resources;
5 **PREPARING** the resources;
6 **CONTROLLING** and organizing the resources to best effect.

**Reflect and Review**

3 The completed puzzle is as follows:

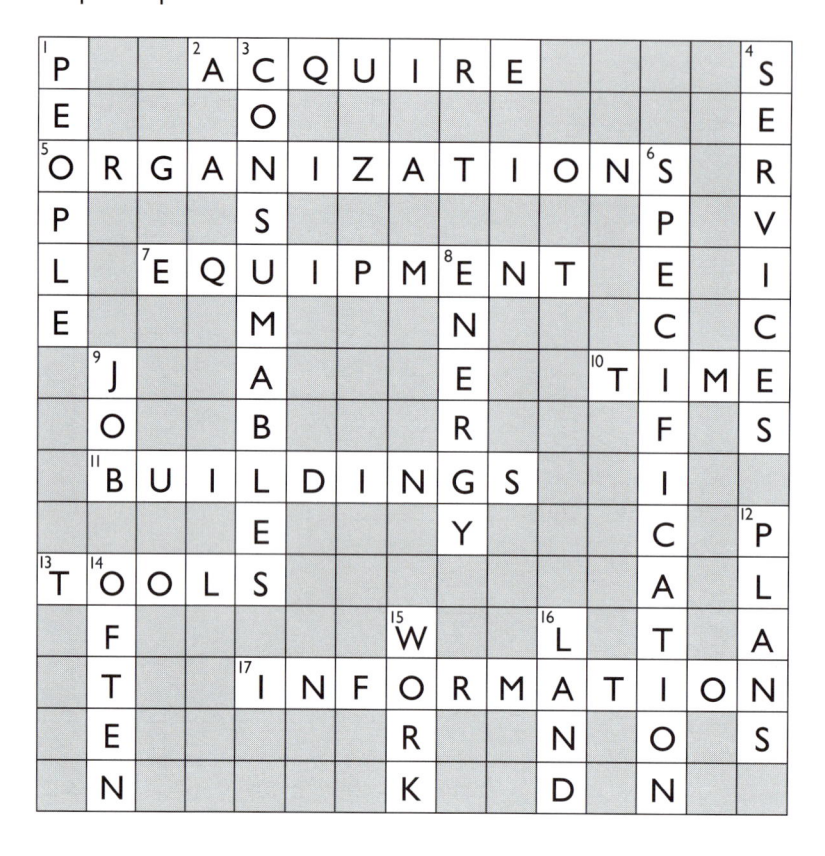

|   | 1 | 2 | 3 | 4 | 5 | 6 | 7 | 8 | 9 | 10 | 11 | 12 | 13 |
|---|---|---|---|---|---|---|---|---|---|----|----|----|----|
| 1 | ¹P |   | ²A | ³C | Q | U | I | R | E |   |   |   | ⁴S |
| 2 | E |   |   | O |   |   |   |   |   |   |   |   | E |
| 3 | ⁵O | R | G | A | N | I | Z | A | T | I | O | ⁶S | R |
| 4 | P |   |   | S |   |   |   |   |   |   |   | P | V |
| 5 | L |   | ⁷E | Q | U | I | P | M | ⁸E | N | T | E | I |
| 6 | E |   |   | M |   |   |   |   | N |   |   | C | C |
| 7 |   | ⁹J |   | A |   |   |   |   | E |   | ¹⁰T | I | M | E |
| 8 |   | O |   | B |   |   |   |   | R |   |   | F | S |
| 9 |   | ¹¹B | U | I | L | D | I | N | G | S |   | I |   |
| 10|   |   |   | E |   |   |   | Y |   |   |   | C | ¹²P |
| 11| ¹³T | ¹⁴O | O | L | S |   |   |   |   |   |   | A | L |
| 12|   | F |   |   |   | ¹⁵W |   | ¹⁶L |   | T | A |
| 13|   | T |   | ¹⁷I | N | F | O | R | M | A | T | I | O | N |
| 14|   | E |   |   |   | R |   | N |   | O | S |
| 15|   | N |   |   |   | K |   | D |   | N |   |

**Self-assessment 2 on pages 53–4**

1 The only reason for holding stock is to have it ready for when it is needed. Because most goods take time to acquire (the lead-time), they may have to be ordered well in advance in order to bridge the gap between the supply and the demand.

2 The completed boxes are as shown.

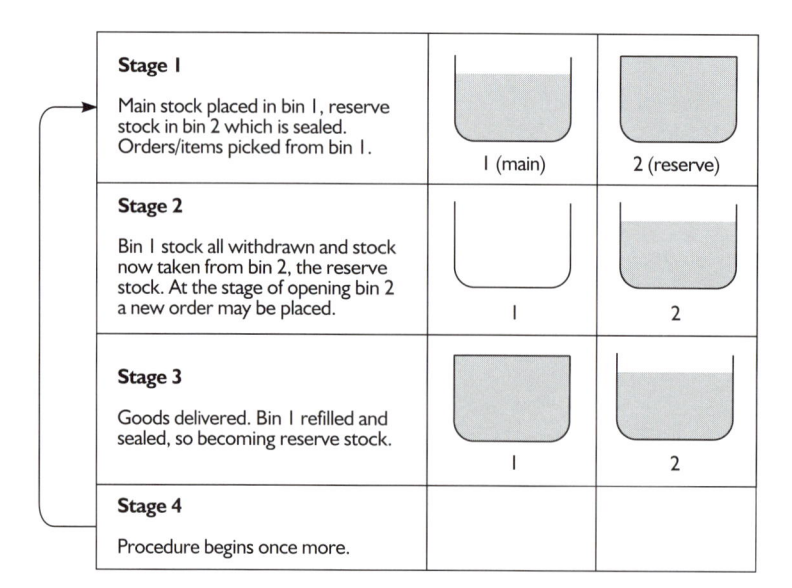

**Stage 1**
Main stock placed in bin 1, reserve stock in bin 2 which is sealed. Orders/items picked from bin 1.

1 (main)    2 (reserve)

**Stage 2**
Bin 1 stock all withdrawn and stock now taken from bin 2, the reserve stock. At the stage of opening bin 2 a new order may be placed.

1    2

**Stage 3**
Goods delivered. Bin 1 refilled and sealed, so becoming reserve stock.

1    2

**Stage 4**
Procedure begins once more.

114

## Reflect and Review

3 The usage values are as follows.

| Item | Unit cost (£) | Annual sales | Usage value (£) |
|---|---|---|---|
| Vacuum cleaner | 230 | 500 | 115,000 |
| Microwave oven | 340 | 750 | 255,000 |
| Refrigerator | 175 | 330 | 57,750 |
| Installing kit | 25 | 1000 | 25,000 |
| Spares kit | 45 | 120 | 5,400 |

4 ABC analysis is a means of categorizing items of stock on the basis of their usage value, where usage value is the cost of the item times the number issued or sold annually. ABC analysis is a modification of the Pareto principle, which shows that the bulk of value is likely to be held by a very small proportion of the total items. When the Pareto principle is applied to stock management, we usually adopt three categories, A, B and C, rather than the two categories of 80 : 20.

5 The completed sentences are as follows.

  a Stock is a **BUFFER** between supply and **DEMAND**, or between the suppliers and the users.
  b Organizations generally aim to keep the **MINIMUM** stocks in the minimum **SPACE** for the minimum time.
  c Having stocks too **HIGH** is bad news; having stocks too **LOW** may be worse news.
  d Opening stock + **PURCHASES** – issues = closing stock.
  e In any store, about **20 PER CENT** of all the items held will account for about **80 PER CENT** of the usage value.

6 a When receiving goods, a goods received note (GRN) is needed. Purchasing need the GRN to check the supplier has delivered the goods ordered. Accounts need the GRN to arrange payment.
  b The minimum stock is the lowest possible level you should hold to avoid running out. The safety stock is lower than the minimum stock. The organization re-orders so that safety stock is not eaten into. However, since it *is* safety stock if, for example, a delivery is unexpectedly late, some safety stock may be used.

# Reflect and Review

**Self-assessment 3 on pages 94–5**

1  The completed diagram is as follows.

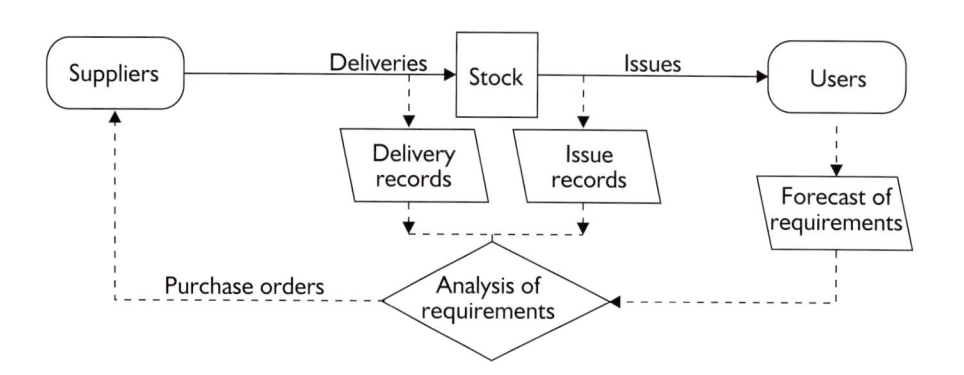

```
Suppliers  ──Deliveries──▶  Stock  ──Issues──▶  Users
    ▲                        │ │                  │
    │                   Delivery Issue            ▼
    │                   records  records    Forecast of
    │                        │ │            requirements
    │                        ▼ ▼                  │
    └──Purchase orders──  Analysis of  ◀──────────┘
                          requirements
```

2  

| | | | |
|---|---|---|---|
| A | Materials requirements planning (MRP) | b | Is concerned with the scheduling of activities and the management of stock. |
| | | e | Produces schedules for activities and purchases as outputs. |
| | | f | Produces forecast stock level as an output. |
| B | Electronic data interchange (EDI) | a | Enables buyers and suppliers to exchange a range of business documents including orders. |
| | | c | Is sometimes known as 'paperless trading'. |
| C | Just-in-time (JIT) | g | Requires suppliers to make frequent deliveries, with very short lead-times. |
| | | h | Enables the customer to minimize stocks held in a waiting area. |
| | | i | Causes the customer's stock-holding costs to be passed to the supplier. |
| D | Automated guided vehicle (AGV) | d | May follow the path of wires laid beneath the floor. |
| | | j | Is typically employed in moving heavy or palleted goods. |

3  a  'Vulnerability' is the intrinsic attraction of a resource to a potential thief. It differs from 'hazard' in that it is almost always impossible to eliminate it in the way that you often can a hazard. Without the 'vulnerability' of items like alcohol, diamonds or electrical goods, there would be no business.

b  For many organisations, the worst security nightmare nowadays is the THEFT or malicious CORRUPTION of ELECTRONIC DATA.

**Reflect and Review**

  c Professional RISK MANAGEMENT approaches are the best means of assuring the security of PERSONNEL STOCK EQUIPMENT and DATA.
  d Having a written Security Policy, made known to all employees, shows everyone that the organisation takes the subject seriously; cares about what happens to employees and their property and that resources will be committed to assuring security based on proper risk assessment.
  e Using the 'what if' question is a simple but effective way of VERIFYING THE EFFECTIVENESS of a risk minimisation strategy.
  f Customers and users of services account for 40 per cent of malicious attacks on PERSONNEL.

# 5 Answers to activities

**Activity 13 on page 31**

Perhaps you didn't have much trouble in answering as follows.

  a  140 (opening stock) + 120 (purchases) – 160 (issues) = 100 (closing stock).
  b  Opening stock + purchases – sales = closing stock.
  c  90 + 60 – 70 = 80.
  d  Opening stock + purchases – closing stock = issues (sales).

# Reflect and Review

**Activity 35 on page 81**

| FIVE-STEP APPROACH TO ASSESSING AND MINIMISING SECURITY RISKS |||||
|---|---|---|---|---|
| **Brief description of situation: Extension to a cash and carry warehouse** <br> During the three-month project, up to 20 contractors' staff will be working on site and will have to gain access via the main staff entrance and existing warehouse. Some overhead work will be involved and at some stage, the contractors will need to break through the existing external wall, close to some high storage racking. The main computer terminal will have to be moved to a new office. It has been agreed that contractors staff can use company fork lift trucks, provided that they are licensed drivers and obtain formal permission from you on every occasion. Of the 50 company staff on site, around 40 are paid in cash on Thursday afternoons. |||||
| | **RESOURCES AFFECTED** ||||
| | HUMAN | STOCK & CASH | EQUIPMENT | DATA |
| 1 Identify resources at risk | Employees, contractors' staff and customers | Stock and cash from tills and payroll | Racking and fork lift trucks <br><br> Computer terminal | Data stored in computer |
| 2 Probability that risk will be realised | Medium to high | Medium to high | Medium | Medium |
| 3 Evaluate consequences | Serious injury or death in 'worst case' scenario | Substantial loss of stock and cash | Serious damage to trucks, buildings, racking and terminal | Serious loss of sensitive data |
| 4 Prioritise consequences | **(1) worst** | **(2) second worst** | **(3) third worst** | **(4) fourth worst** |
| 5 Recommended strategy to eliminate or minimise the risks (tackling the 'worst first') | (1) Agree safety plan with contractors. Agree supervisory arrangements and site liaison for contractors and their employees or sub-contractors. Check and upgrade first aid arrangements as necessary. <br> (2) Demand verification of contractors' staff backgrounds. Agree search procedures for contractors' vehicles and personnel. Upgrade security checks for stock and cash. Impose 'unbreakable rules' for access to site and 'signing in and out' of contractors' employees, identified by badges/lapel badges with photographs etc. <br> (3) Agree strict 'ground rules' for checking fork lift truck licenses; identification of holders (e.g. lapel badges). Clear procedures regarding the misuse of equipment, including summary dismissal from site. <br> (4) Schedule computer move at best (quietest) moment available. Check on electrical works. Ensure back up systems working and constantly up-to-date ||||

# 6 Answers to the quick quiz

Answer 1  You could have mentioned: people; equipment; land; buildings; finance; materials; information; energy; time.

Answer 2  The simple answer is that people do not respond well when they feel they are being treated like a piece of furniture or equipment. Managers who fall into this trap seldom succeed in their aims.

Answer 3  To get the optimum value from equipment, it is important for the people using it to have: a good understanding of what it is designed to do; training in how to use it; a proper system of maintenance; an appropriate system of security.

Answer 4  Raw materials are basic substances that are processed in order to manufacture products, such as wood and plastics. Components are parts, often having themselves been manufactured from raw materials, which go to make a larger assembly. Consumables are items that are used up in a work process, and do not necessarily form part of the final product.

Answer 5  If stocks are too high, money is tied up in goods that aren't being used. If stocks are too low, the organization's activities may be impeded, which may be potentially even more costly.

Answer 6  Shrinkage is losses and deterioration caused by: a decline in quality; goods becoming out of date; damage; pilferage.

Answer 7  The book stock formula is expressed as follows:
$$\text{opening stock} + \text{purchases} - \text{issues} = \text{closing stock}$$

Answer 8  ABC analysis is a method of determining the relative amount of attention that should be given to goods in stock. (You might also have mentioned that a usage value is calculated for each item, which is the purchase price times the number issued or sold; the highest usage value items receive the greatest amount of attention.)

Answer 9  There are two possible transactions involved in the receipt of goods: taking in new goods, just delivered by a supplier; and taking back old goods, which had been issued and which are now being returned for some reason.

Answer 10  The minimum stock is the lowest possible level you should hold to avoid any danger of running out.

Answer 11  There are real advantages to having purchasing specialists, including the facts that: it is a job requiring a good deal of expertise; it is important to build up good

## Reflect and Review

Answer 12
: relationships with regular suppliers, and this takes time and effort; a specialist will be able to find suppliers for new items quickly; non-specialist managers won't waste time on purchasing tasks, which they have no training in.

Answer 12
: Potential advantages include: lower inventory costs, lower handling costs, lower space costs, and increased productivity. Disadvantages are that it may be difficult to implement unless your organization has a lot of 'buying power', a great deal of planning is required, and if things ever go wrong, business may effectively come to a halt.

Answer 13
: Inputs are: the master schedule (a forecast or actual demand for products or services); a bill of requirements (a list of all parts, materials, and services required for each product); the opening stock balances; a schedule of capacity (what the organization is capable of producing). Outputs are: an activity schedule (what has to be done); a purchase schedule (what has to be bought); a shortage list; forecast stock levels; forecast of spare or deficient capacity.

Answer 14
: That information is not given to people who will not have to use it in the work which they do. The principle should be applied throughout the 'hierarchy' of an organisation to protect confidential information which might fall into the hands of a competitor.

Answer 15
: It is not legally or morally acceptable to reject expensive security measures when the LIVES and LIMBS of people are involved.

Answer 15
: There are many sites to which large numbers of members of the general public and employees have to have general access, making it difficult to keep them away from any but the most sensitive areas. Even without that constraint, such a policy is still only as good as the people who work in the areas, who must unfailingly challenge 'strangers' or people not having the correct identification, however important they may look.

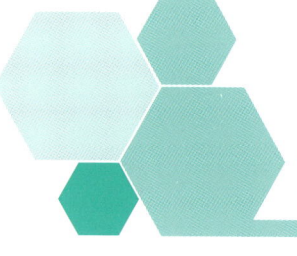

# 7 Certificate

Completion of this certificate by an authorized person shows that you have worked through all the parts of this workbook and satisfactorily completed the assessments. The certificate provides a record of what you have done that may be used for exemptions or as evidence of prior learning against other nationally certificated qualifications.

Pergamon Flexible Learning and ILM are always keen to refine and improve their products. One of the key sources of information to help this process are people who have just used the product. If you have any information or views, good or bad, please pass these on.

# INSTITUTE OF LEADERSHIP & MANAGEMENT

# SUPERSERIES

## Controlling Physical Resources

..................................................................................................................

has satisfactorily completed this workbook

Name of signatory ..................................................................................................

Position ..................................................................................................................

Signature ................................................................................................................

Date ........................................................................

Official stamp

Fourth Edition

# INSTITUTE OF LEADERSHIP & MANAGEMENT
# SUPERSERIES
## FOURTH EDITION

| | |
|---|---|
| Achieving Quality | 0 7506 5874 6 |
| Appraising Performance | 0 7506 5838 X |
| Becoming More Effective | 0 7506 5887 8 |
| Budgeting for Better Performance | 0 7506 5880 0 |
| Caring for the Customer | 0 7506 5840 1 |
| Collecting Information | 0 7506 5888 6 |
| Commitment to Equality | 0 7506 5893 2 |
| Controlling Costs | 0 7506 5842 8 |
| Controlling Physical Resources | 0 7506 5886 X |
| Delegating Effectively | 0 7506 5816 9 |
| Delivering Training | 0 7506 5870 3 |
| Effective Meetings at Work | 0 7506 5882 7 |
| Improving Efficiency | 0 7506 5871 1 |
| Information in Management | 0 7506 5890 8 |
| Leading Your Team | 0 7506 5839 8 |
| Making a Financial Case | 0 7506 5892 4 |
| Making Communication Work | 0 7506 5875 4 |
| Managing Change | 0 7506 5879 7 |
| Managing Lawfully – Health, Safety and Environment | 0 7506 5841 X |
| Managing Lawfully – People and Employment | 0 7506 5853 3 |
| Managing Relationships at Work | 0 7506 5891 6 |
| Managing Time | 0 7506 5877 0 |
| Managing Tough Times | 0 7506 5817 7 |
| Marketing and Selling | 0 7506 5837 1 |
| Motivating People | 0 7506 5836 3 |
| Networking and Sharing Information | 0 7506 5885 1 |
| Organizational Culture and Context | 0 7506 5884 3 |
| Organizational Environment | 0 7506 5889 4 |
| Planning and Controlling Work | 0 7506 5813 4 |
| Planning Training and Development | 0 7506 5860 6 |
| Preventing Accidents | 0 7506 5835 5 |
| Project and Report Writing | 0 7506 5876 2 |
| Securing the Right People | 0 7506 5822 3 |
| Solving Problems | 0 7506 5818 5 |
| Storing and Retrieving Information | 0 7506 5894 0 |
| Understanding Change | 0 7506 5878 9 |
| Understanding Finance | 0 7506 5815 0 |
| Understanding Quality | 0 7506 5881 9 |
| Working In Teams | 0 7506 5814 2 |
| Writing Effectively | 0 7506 5883 5 |

To order – phone us direct for prices and availability details
(please quote ISBNs when ordering) on 01865 888190